The Practical Past

The FlashPoints series is devoted to books that consider literature beyond strictly national and disciplinary frameworks, and that are distinguished both by their historical grounding and by their theoretical and conceptual strength. Our books engage theory without losing touch with history and work historically without falling into uncritical positivism. FlashPoints aims for a broad audience within the humanities and the social sciences concerned with moments of cultural emergence and transformation. In a Benjaminian mode, FlashPoints is interested in how literature contributes to forming new constellations of culture and history and in how such formations function critically and politically in the present. Series titles are available online at http://escholarship.org/uc/flashpoints.

A complete list of titles begins on p. 118.

The Practical Past

Hayden White

NORTHWESTERN UNIVERSITY PRESS | EVANSTON, ILLINOIS

Northwestern University Press
www.nupress.northwestern.edu

Digital Printing

Library of Congress Cataloging-in-Publication Data

White, Hayden V., 1928–, author.
The practical past / Hayden White.
pages cm — (Flashpoints)
ISBN 978-0-8101-3006-7 (pbk. : alk. paper)
1. Literature and history. 2. Literature, Modern—History and criticism. 3. History, Modern—20th century—Historiography. I. Title. II. Series: FlashPoints (Evanston, Ill.)
PN50.W486 2014
809.93358—dc23

2014018902

To my beloved Margaret, without whom I could not have imagined a life in art

Contents

Preface ix

1. The Practical Past 3
2. Truth and Circumstance: What (if Anything) Can Properly Be Said about the Holocaust? 25
3. The Historical Event 41
4. Contextualism and Historical Understanding 63
5. Historical Discourse and Literary Theory 75

Afterword 97

Notes 105

Preface

All my life I have been interested in the relationship between history and literature. This relationship has interested me since the time I first became fascinated by history. Like many historians, I first encountered the historical past in the stories of knights in arms, kings, crusades, and battles; tales of Robin Hood, Roland, and King Arthur; the Norse myths, Greek myths, and, of course, the history of Rome. In those days, the distinction between history and fiction was dissolved in the thrill of narrativity and the magic of an animation which would later be found in the movies where, once again, "history" was presented in the images of heroes and heroines, nobility and villainy, magi and sorcerers, and, of course, love and passion. I did not mistake the tales told in books and films (and of course, the comics) for reality, and now I think that this was because I understood, tacitly if not consciously, that, being tales about the past, they could not possibly be of the same reality as that which made up the present.

I was fortunate enough to study history at university under one of the great teachers of his generation, William J. Bossenbrook, who taught us that history was primarily a story of the clash of ideas, values, and dreams (rather than of bodies and machines only), and that dialectical relationships obtain only between concepts, not things. Thus, while a radical politics may be related to a conservative politics in the manner of an opposition, in which the one defines its own positivity as the negation of what it takes to be the negativity of its opposite, the relationship between two things (a book, say, and a hammer) cannot be so construed. There is no way that one could conceive a hammer to be the *contrary*, let alone the *contradictory*, of a book. And the same can be said of the relationship of equivalency out of which Marx made such grand hay in his discussion of the fetishism of gold in the introduction to *Das Kapital*.

And so too for communities or societies. They may regard themselves as related by opposition or negation to some other community or society and indeed may act in such a way as to become merely an "other" of some "other," but in reality they are only *different* from one another. In large part, Bossenbrook taught me, history is the story of communities—nations, social groups, families, and so on—defining themselves as opposed to their others, when in reality there are only differences among them. He taught me to value individuality over both difference and opposition; indeed, that insofar as there is "history," there are only individuals—singular or collective, as the case may be. And that finally, insofar as there are only individuals in history, history itself must remain a mystery to be pondered more than a puzzle to be solved. As in Maimonides's conception of the proper way to study Holy Writ, the aim of historical writing was to increase perplexity rather than dispel it.

What has all of this to do with the relation between history and literature? Most immediately it has to do with the fact that the term "history" is the signifier of a concept rather than a *reference* to a thing or domain of being having material presence. This concept may have as its signified either "the past" or something like "temporal process" but these, too, are concepts rather than things. Neither has material presence. Both are known only by way of "traces" or material entities which indicate not so much what the things that produced them were, as, rather, the fact that "some thing" passed by a certain place or did something in that place. What it was that had passed by or what it had done in that place will remain a mystery, the solution to which may be inferred or intuited, but the nature of which must remain conjectural—indeed, must remain a possibility only and therefore a "fiction."

By fiction I mean a construction or conjecture about "what possibly happened" or might happen at some time and some place, in the present, in the past, or indeed even in the future. Defense of this position would require forays into ontology and epistemology, not to speak of the ethics and aesthetics of historical writing for which this is not the occasion. My own position has to do with the familiar considerations about the conditions of possibility of a scientific knowledge of "the historical past," namely the fact that *past* events, processes, institutions, persons, and things are no longer perceivable nor directly knowable in the way that present or still living entities are. Thus, a correspondence theory of historical truth fails by way of the fallacy of misplaced concreteness. Secondly, although modern professional historians limit themselves to assertions about the past that can be derived from the study of documents, monuments, and other traces of the past's reality, the kind of study of such evidence licensed by the historical profession is so *ad hoc*, merely commonsensical, and fragmentary that not even the criterion of coherence can be met without a great deal of patching up that is of a figurative (and therefore fiction-making) kind. The idea that the relationships among things (rather than concepts) are logically coherent and *therefore* reflective of the reality of the things supposedly so related and of the relationships among them—all this is too metaphysically idealistic to be credited in modernity.

Mine is a relativist position, I am quite aware. But I do not see how the truth of our knowledge of the past or more specifically the historical past—not to mention their meaning—could be assessed other than relative to the cultural presuppositions of those who made them and in the light of the cultural presuppositions of those who wish to assess them. This is not an argument for universal relativism, since I am perfectly willing to accept the criteria of both correspondence and coherence as ways of assessing the truth of knowledge about entities still open to ostensive indication and direct perception and those which are in principle "reproducible" under laboratory and experimental conditions. Since historical entities are by definition individuals, they are what in British English is called "one-off" entities, neither reproducible experimentally nor directly perceivable since, also by definition, they are "past." (The trace of the past which perdures into the present is another matter. It is by definition not past at all even though it bears marks or indices of past actions or acts or processes.)

So I accept the constructionist position with respect to historical knowledge for reasons both theoretical (given above in outline) and practical, which is to say, in the extent to which it allows me to provide an account—on pragmatist grounds—of the complex interrelationships among what is called historical reality (the past), historical writing, and what used to be called "fiction" but which I now wish to call (following Marie-Laure Ryan) "literary writing."[1]

Literary writing is a mode of language-use distinct from utilitarian or communicative (message) writing, by virtue of the dominance in it of the *poetic function* of speech. The idea of literary writing (as against "literature") permits me to refine the distinction between history (or historical writing) and fiction (or imaginative writing) and overcome the belief that they are *opposed* to one another as mutually exclusive alternatives. It is only if fiction is identified with writing about imaginary beings and literature identified with fiction that the relation between history and literature must be seen as little more than an opposition between the real world (past and present) and fantasy, dreams, daydreams, and other similarly phantasmatic activities (illusions, delusions, phobias, and so on). The notion of literary writing not only allows us to utilize the idea of "poetry" or more specifically "the poetic" in a technical and analytical sense but also to subsume fiction as a *species* of the genus "literature" rather than view it (fiction) as the essence of substance of all things literary. For not all literary writing is fictional any more than all fictional writing is necessarily literary. Biography and autobiography, travel and anthropological writing may be "literary" though not fictional, while certain kinds of imaginative writing, such as science fantasy, "chick lit," *telenovelas*, advertising, and so on will be fictional though not necessarily literary. In other words, some fictional writing is literary in the sense of having the poetic function as its dominant, while some other fictional writing—formulaic, stilted, or simply algorithmic—is anything but literary because the poetic function is lacking or nil.

In some of my past essays, I have frequently spoken of history-writing as a mixture of fact and fiction and on other occasions even suggested that history-writing—especially of the narrative kind—could best be understood as literature and therefore as fiction. This was misleading because I had failed to make clear that by the term "fiction" I had had in mind Jeremy Bentham's conception of it, as a kind of invention or construction based on hypothesis rather than a manner of writing or thinking focused on purely imaginary or fantastic entities. Actually, however, the relationship between history and literature is that which obtains between two species (genres, modes) of written discourse, historiography, historical prose, or writing about "history" and imaginative literary writing in general. "In general," because historiography is a genre of writing which belongs to the category or class of artistic prose discourses.

Of course, not all historical writing is or aspires to be "artistic" in the way that a poem or memoir or a novel would do. Indeed, since the early nineteenth century, most historical writing has defined its claim to "objectivity" by its repudiation of any of the more recognizable devices of rhetoric or the patterning techniques of poetic diction. And this even while it purported still to "tell stories" about "what happened in the past" and continued to suggest that the truths of history were best conveyed in the idiom of well-told narratives. So let me make clear on this occasion that, as far as I am concerned, the past is made up of events and entities which once existed but no longer do; that historians properly believe that this past can be accessed and made sense of by studying the traces of this past existing in the present; and that, finally, the historical past consists of the referents of those aspects of the past studied and then represented (or presented) in the genres of writings which, by convention, are called "histories" and are recognized to be such by professional scholars *licensed* to decide what is "properly" historical and what is not.

Having said this and effectively yielded some theoretical ground to the professional historians' conviction that "history" and "historicality" are whatever practicing historians considered them to be, I must now point out (and here I follow the lead of the late Michael Oakeshott) that what is called "the historical past" is a *construction* and only a highly selective *version* of the past understood as the totality of all the events and entities that once existed but no longer exist and most of which have left no evidence of their existence.[2] This is why, of course, historians have always had to specify a subject-of-history: the state, the nation, a class, a place or site, an institution, and so on about which a factual (as against an imaginary) story can be told.

In other words, the historical past has to be distinguished from the past as a constantly changing whole or totality of which it (the historical past) is only a part.

Oakeshott has suggested that in addition to the whole past and the historical past we must take account of what he calls "the practical past" of particular persons, groups, institutions, and agencies—that is to say, the past that people as individuals or members of groups draw upon in order to help them make assessments and make decisions in ordinary everyday life as well as in extreme situations (such as catastrophes, disasters, battles, judicial and other kinds of conflicts in which survival is at issue). It can easily be seen that in practical life, the historical past and knowledge of that past are of little or any use. Indeed, professional historians profess to be interested primarily if not exclusively in "the historical past in itself" alone, or in understanding the past on its own terms, and resisting any inclination to draw inferences of a practical or utilitarian kind from the past to the present. Moreover, it is generally believed that when the professional historian uses his expertise to promote some present institution or authority (such as the nation, the state, the church, and so on), he will have inevitably violated the rules of objectivity and disinterestedness that are the mark of his professionalism as a scholar.

Professional historians' accounts of the past have typically claimed authority to identify and neutralize ideological distortions of the past intended to promote belief in a given political or social program in the present by virtue of the kind of objectivity and disinterest that a proper professional historiography will manifest. So whatever else modern scientific historical investigation may purport to be, it can be of service to the practical life of the present only in the extent to which it can correct or neutralize or dissolve the distortions, myths, and illusions about the past generated by interests of a predominantly practical kind. This is why there is a fundamental conflict between the historical past and the practical past in modern enlightened (secular or a-religious) societies. But this is also why such societies require a way of explicating the practical past which, while dealing with what is commonly called "history," utilizes techniques of description, analysis, and presentation that resemble those cultivated by professional historians primarily in form (the narrative) rather than in content (factual information).

In modern Western societies, the principal genre of discourse developed for this purpose (among others) has been the modern, realistic novel, the distinctive attribute of which (as Erich Auerbach argued) was that it took "history" as its main and ultimate referent. But in the modern realistic novel, the "history" alluded to by Auerbach is that "practical past" which professional historians have ruled out as a possible object of investigation because it is not amenable to a properly scientific or objective treatment.

The practical past, however, *is* amenable to a literary—which is to say, an artistic or poetic—treatment that is anything but "fictional" in the sense of being purely imaginary or fantastic in kind. A literary treatment of the past—as displayed in various instances of the modern(ist) novel (but also in poetic and dramatic discourse)—has the real past as its ultimate referent (what, in discourse theory, is referred to as "the substance of its content"), but focuses on those aspects of the real past which the historical past cannot deal with.

For example, politics of the past is a conventional object of historical investigation, not only because it is an important element of a community's life but also because it produces the kind of documentary evidence that permits a properly historical reconstruction of its evolution. It is quite otherwise with a topic like love or work or suffering and the kinds of relationships among them which are (or were) real enough but which are accessible as objects of *practical* study only by way of imaginative hypothesization. The kind of presentation of the "mood" or atmosphere of post-Holocaust Europe found in W. G. Sebald's *Austerlitz* or of post–World War II, Newark, New Jersey, in Philip Roth's *American Pastoral* is nonetheless "historical" for being an imaginative rather than an exclusively evidentiary construction. Neither of these two works is properly classifiable as "fiction" although both are written in a manner manifestly "literary." Their ultimate referents are "history" even if their manifest form (their "substance of expression") is imaginary. They are both perfect examples of the uses that can be made of "the practical past."

H.W.
Santa Cruz, California

The Practical Past

CHAPTER 1

The Practical Past

Near the beginning of W. G. Sebald's "novel," *Austerlitz*, we are introduced to the book's eponymous protagonist, "Jacques Austerlitz," by the narrator who has journeyed to "Belgium" and specifically to "Antwerp"—"partly for study purposes, partly for other reasons which were never entirely clear"—and has ended up in the waiting room of the central railway station (the "Salle des pas perdus") where he encounters Austerlitz taking pictures of the waiting room and engages him in conversation about the history of architecture, which happens to be Austerlitz's profession. Thus began, the story has it, in the year 1967, a series of encounters between the narrator and Austerlitz who, it turns out, is searching for information about his family who, he had discovered only at the age of sixteen, were Czech Jews who may (or may not) have perished in the death camps of the Third Reich. The novel relates the many accidental and planned encounters between the narrator and Austerlitz from that first meeting in the "Salle des pas perdus" in Antwerp's Central Station down to a final meeting in Gare d'Austerlitz in Paris where Jacques Austerlitz relates to the narrator the ways by which the past is able to hide its secrets from the living, even to the point of destroying the monuments attesting the existence of a past (as in the newly built Bibliothèque nationale in Paris: "this gigantic new library, which, according to one of the loathsome phrases now current is supposed to serve as the treasure house of our entire literary heritage, proved useless in my search for any traces of my father who had disappeared from Paris more than fifty years ago.") It is not clear whether Austerlitz objects to the inutility of the new Bibliothèque nationale or is simply lamenting the loss of the old one. In any event, Jacques Austerlitz's quest for the identity and traces of his parents takes the form of a journey in space, from one "lieu de memoir" to another; each of them manifests another aspect of how what had once been presented as a "heritage" can be shown to be a kind of impediment to useful knowledge of the past. The ultimate destination (or rather the penultimate one) is Theresienstadt's famous Potemkin village concentration camp where the transit point to the death camps was given the public face of a vacation spa like Marienbad. This masquerade of a concentration camp as a fancy retirement community provides a kind of image of fulfillment for all of the places of Europe wherein the good old values of humanism and Christianity, of the nation and the community, of the state and the church are allowed to appear as little more than "zoological gardens" in which hapless captured animals look out listlessly at the human visitors who think they occupy zones of freedom and responsibility.

Right at the beginning of *Austerlitz*, the narrator (before encountering Austerlitz in the Central Station in Antwerp) visits the "Nocturama" of the Antwerp zoo. The Nocturama is an enclosure for animals which sleep during the day and come out only at night and whose eyes are unseeing in daylight but percipient in darkness. The narrator opens his account of his meeting with Austerlitz in a meditation on the eyes of animals which can see only in the dark and likens them to the eyes of philosophers, such as Wittgenstein (a picture of whose eyes appears in the text), who teach us to see in images rather than in concepts. This section is followed by a long account, first of the proportions and decorations of the waiting room in Antwerp's Central Station, and next of the structure, appearance, and history of a series of military fortifications built around Antwerp which went from being utterly ineffectual in defense of the city (and being expanded and augmented with every failure until they became so extensive that they could not be manned) to their use as a Gestapo prison and torture facility during the Second World War. The fortifications of Fort Breendonk serve as a kind of master metaphor of Sebald's narrator's report of Jacques Austerlitz's journey across post-World War II Europe in his effort to use his expert historical knowledge to establish his own identity or at least that aspect of it that might come with knowledge of his origins.

If *Austerlitz* is, as the cover of the German edition informs us, a "*Roman*" (novel), it is one in which nothing very much happens, which lacks anything remotely resembling a plot or plot structure (the "failed quest" novel?), and in which everything would seem to turn, in Henry James fashion, on "character," except that, in the cases of both Austerlitz and his narrator, the notion of "character" itself explodes into the shards and fragments of "men without properties." And yet, the book is chock-full of interesting not to say fascinating historical information, lore, and knowledge. The narrator stages Austerlitz's expertise in his professional field (art history) in a convincing manner, and his descriptions of the various historical monuments and sites (*lieux*) of famous historical events are utterly "realistic" in the common meaning of that term. The meaning of this *Roman* emerges in the interstices of the successive descriptions of places and edifices that attest to the ways in which "civilization" has been built on the structures of evil, incarceration, exclusion, destruction, and the kind of humiliation endured by that little raccoon which, in the pale light of the Nocturama, "sat beside a little stream with a serious expression on its face, washing the same piece of apple over and over again, as if it hoped ("als offe er") that all this washing, which went far beyond any reasonable thoroughness ("weit über jede vernünftige Gründlichkeit"), would help it to escape the unreal world ("aus der falschen Welt") in which it had arrived, so to speak, through no fault of its own ("ohne sein eigenes Zutun")."[1] (English ed., p. 4 / German ed., pp. 10–11)

The predominance in Sebald's book of real-world—which is to say, historical, empirical, and documentable—"fact" makes it difficult to classify it as "fiction." "Literature" or literary writing it certainly is; it is as self-consciously "fashioned" and assertive of its "techniques" as any recognizably "poetic" artifact could be. At the same time, all this artifice is being used to give access to a real, historical referent: what Benjamin might recognize as an account of what our vaunted "civilization" owes for its benefits and advantages to modern man's peculiar forms of cruelty to its own kind. In other words, the literary devices disposed by Sebald in *Austerlitz* serve to produce a *literary* lens by which to justify a judgment (ethical or moral in kind) on a real world of historical fact. It has to be said that there is no "argument" that we might extract from the book regarding the "true" nature of the historical world thus displayed before us by means of the narrator's account of the "fictional" quest of Jacques Austerlitz for information about his "fictional" parents. Or rather that, if there is an argument to be extracted from it, it is one that can only be inferred from the way the events reported over the course of the (non) action are encoded figuratively. To be sure, every narrative or every account of a series of events related in a narrativizing manner, which is to say, given the shape and form of a story, can be translated into an apparatus purely conceptual in nature, after the manner in which George Lakoff treats all metaphorical statements (i.e., as masked concepts).[2] But it has to be stressed that what gives to Sebald's account of a real historical world the aspect of fictionality is precisely the way he resists any impulse to conceptualize either his narrator's role or the "meaning" of his protagonist's "imaginary" journey in search of a lost origin.

On the other hand, this book is manifestly *not* a history even though its "content" and its ultimate referent are manifestly "the historical," which means, one might argue, that the book, quite apart from the melancholy which arises from the suggestion that a merely "historical" knowledge of "history" will raise more problems than it solves, is less than helpful when it is a matter of seeking a meaning for an individual life or existence. Again, as with Walter Benjamin, the story of Jacques Austerlitz's inquiry into the recent past of Europe seems to reveal only that the people who have "made history" were—like the Nazis—as much interested in hiding evidence of their deeds as they were in celebrating and monumentalizing their intentions. It turns out that, if we can draw any lessons from contemplation of the Austerlitz story, there is no such thing as a "history" against which we could measure and assess the validity of what Amos Funkenstein calls "antihistory," by which he meant "mythifications" intended to cover over and obscure the "truths" of proper historiography. It is all antihistory, always written as much "against" as well as on behalf of the (official) "truth."

So maybe we might classify *Austerlitz* as a historical novel, a kind of postmodernist version of the genre invented (so the legend has it) by Sir Walter Scott and brought to consummation in Tolstoy's *War and Peace*, which, so it seems to me, at once consummates and "deconstructs" the genre of the historical novel as it had been cultivated at the hands of Scott, Manzoni, Dumas, Hugo, Dickens, George Eliot, Flaubert, and God knows how many others in the nineteenth century in Europe.[3] We could say that, except for the fact that *Austerlitz* can be read as an allegory of the impossibility of—or, to cite Nietzsche—the disadvantage (*Nachteil*) of history "für das Leben." As thus envisaged, Sebald's "novel" can be viewed as a contribution in a peculiarly postmodernist mode to that discussion over the relation between history and literature, or factual and fictional writing, or realistic and imaginative writing, or rational and mythical writing opened up by the so-called "crisis of historism" (*Historismus*) in the early twentieth century. And if our purpose were to enter into that discussion we would have to account for the fact that the genre of the historical novel in the time of Scott, Goethe, and Byron enjoyed virtually universal popularity among the literate public while, at the same time, enduring universal contemnation at the hands of professional historians who regarded its mixture of fact with fiction, its constitutive anachronism, and its attempt to examine the past by the instruments of imagination as a crime not to say a sin of Mosaic amplitude—"Thou shalt not mix the kinds." The fact is that the authority and prestige of this literary genre waned with the constitution of a new kind of science in the late nineteenth century, underwent a mindbending transformation at the hands of the great literary modernists (Joyce, Pound, Eliot, Stein, Proust, Kafka, Woolf, etc.), only to be revived in a different mode and register by virtually every writer that we might wish to praise or condemn with the label "postmodernist." As Linda Hutcheon and Amy Elias have demonstrated (to my satisfaction, at least) the dominant genre of postmodernist writing is "historiographic metafiction" (Hutcheon) or simply "metahistorical romance" (Elias).

It has to be said that the rebirth of the historical novel in the forms given it by writers as different as Thomas Pynchon (*The Crying of Lot 49*, *V.*, *Mason & Dixon*), Don DeLillo (*Libra*, *Underworld*), Philip Roth (*American Pastoral*, *The Plot against America*), the Israeli writer Michal Govrin (*Snapshots*), Robert Rosenstone (*King of Odessa*), Norman Mailer, William Gass (*The Tunnel*), Cormac McCarthy, Pat Barker, J. M. Coetzee, Jonathan Safran Foer, and so on has to be set within the context of the post–World War II discussion of Nazi crimes against humanity, the genocide of the Jews, Gypsies, homosexuals, and the mentally disabled—the whole question of the meaning and significance of the Holocaust, the felt need to "come to terms with the past," not only in Europe but also in the rest of the colonial world, the demand by the casualties, victims, and survivors of new kinds of events made possible by the very science and culture that had allowed the West to destroy what it could not colonize, incarcerate, domesticate, intimidate, or otherwise humble and humiliate. This widespread effort to "come to terms with the past" involved not only the uncovering of what had been ignored, suppressed, repressed, or otherwise hidden from view in the past of nations, classes, races, and, yes, genders, too. It also entailed or seemed to many to entail the necessity of thinking once more about the utility, the worth or value, the advantages and disadvantages of the kind of knowledge of the past produced by the new cadres of professional historians that had been established in the late nineteenth century for service to the European nation-state but which also laid claim to the status of a "science" (*Wissenschaft*) and were charged with determining what kinds of questions could be asked by the present of the past, what kind of evidence could be adduced in any effort to ask the proper questions, what constituted properly "historical" answers to those questions, and where the line was to be drawn for distinguishing between a proper and an improper use of historical "knowledge" in any effort to clarify or illuminate contemporary efforts to answer central questions of moral and societal concern: what Kant called the "practical" (by which he meant the ethical) question, what should I (we) do?

Now, it is here that I come to the subject of "the practical past." I had to approach it through a discussion of the historical novel, of postmodernist literary writing, and of Sebald's particular take on history and the historical, in order to be able to say something worthwhile about that statement of de Certeau that I have used for my epigraph: "Fiction is the repressed other of history." My argument will be that one of the ways that history in the early nineteenth century succeeded in constituting itself as a scientific (or parascientific) discipline was by detaching historio*graphy* from its millennial association with rhetoric and, after that, belles lettres, an activity of amateurs and dilettantes, a kind of writing that was more "creative" or "poetic," in which the imagination, intuition, passion, and, yes, even prejudice were permitted to take precedence over considerations of veracity, perspicuity, "plain" speech, and common sense. So, *à bas a la rhetorique*! This, Victor Hugo's sentiment, was shared by the proponents of what would come to be called "the realist novel," most prominently by Gustave Flaubert whose own brand of realism took the form of a disparagement of rhetoric on behalf of what he called "style." But the exclusion of rhetoric (considered as a theory of composition by which a certain body of information was worked up for different practical uses, persuasion, incitement to action, inspiration of feelings of reverence or repulsion, etc.) from historiology had an effect on historical studies quite different from what a similar exclusion of rhetoric from "literary writing" will have had on "literature."

The older, rhetorically structured mode of historical writing openly promoted the study and contemplation of the past as propaedeutic to a life in the public sphere, as an alternative ground to theology and metaphysics (not to mention as an alternative to the kind of knowledge one might derive from experience of what Aristotle called the "banausic" life of commerce and trade), for the discovery or invention of principles by which to answer the central question of ethics: "What should (ought, must) I do?" Or to put it in Lenin's terms: "What is to be done?"

The professionalization of historical studies required in principle at least that the past be studied, as it was said, "for itself alone" or as "a thing in itself," without any ulterior motive other than a desire for the truth (of fact, to be sure, rather than doctrine) about the past and without any inclination to draw lessons from the study of the past and import them into the present in order to justify actions and programs for the future. In other words, history in its status as a science for the study of the past purported to purge the study of the past of any ethical content—while, at the same time, serving the nation-state as custodian of its genealogy. Thus, while purporting to study "the historical past," historiography in its scientific form was serving the needs and interests of "the practical past."

What is the practical past? The concept comes from some of the late writings of the political philosopher Michael Oakeshott, and it refers to those notions of "the past" which all of us carry around with us in our daily lives and which we draw upon, willy-nilly and as best we can, for information, ideas, models, formulas, and strategies for solving all the practical problems—from personal affairs to grand political programs—met with in whatever we conceive to be our present "situation." We draw upon this past without much self-consciousness when it comes to practical matters, such as recalling how to start the car, how to do long division, how to cook an omelette, and so on. But this practical past is also the past of repressed memory, dream, and desire as much as it is of problem-solving, strategy, and tactics of living, both personal and communal.

Oakeshott invokes the concept of the practical past in contrast to what he calls "the historical past," that past built up by modern professional historians as the corrected and organized version of that part of the whole past which has been established as having actually existed on the basis of evidence authenticated by other historians as admissible in history's court of appeal. The historical past is a theoretically motivated construction, existing only in the books and articles published by professional historians; it is constructed as an end in itself, possesses little or no value for understanding or explaining the present, and provides no guidelines for acting in the present or foreseeing the future. Nobody ever actually lived or experienced the historical past because it could not have been apprehended on the basis of whatever it was that past agents knew, thought, or imagined about their world during *their* present.

Historians, viewing the past from the vantage point of a future state of affairs, can claim a knowledge about the past present that no past agent in his present could ever have possessed.

This was not always the case, of course. Historical writing in its origins was supposed to teach lessons and provide models of comportment for living human beings especially in the prosecution of public affairs. And this remained the case well into the eighteenth century. But in the nineteenth century, the study of history ceased to have any practical utility precisely in the extent to which it succeeded in transforming into a science. Historians could tell you what the properly processed evidence licenses you to believe about what happened in given parts of the historical past, but they could not tell you how to deal with your present situation or solve your current practical problems. In present situations, where judgment and decision are called for, the only part of the past that is useful is the one which Reinhart Koselleck called "the space of experience" (*Erfahrungsraum*), that warehouse of archived memories, ideas, dreams, and values which we go to as a kind of "old curiosity shop" in search of intimations of where we came from in order to grasp, in some way, what we are to do with all the detritus left to us as a legacy of dubious relevance to the solution of current "practical" problems.

Here the term "practical" is to be understood in Kant's sense as born of the uniquely human awareness of the *necessity* of doing something. We call upon the practical past of memory, dream, fantasy, experience, and imagination when confronted with the question: "What ought I (or we) do?" The historical past cannot help us here, because the most it can tell us is what people in *other* times, places, and circumstances did in their situation at *that* time and place. This information contains no warrant for deducing what we, in our situation, in our time and our place, *should* do in order to conform to the standard set by that categorical imperative which licenses our belief in the possibility of morality itself.

Now, in what follows, I am going to try to develop some of the implications of Oakeshott's distinction between the practical past and the historical past in order to try to theorize a problem that has bedeviled philosophy of history since the beginning of history's transformation from its status as a discourse to its status as a (putative) science. This problem arose in the early nineteenth century when, in order to constitute itself as a science, history had to be detached and differentiated from its former habitation in rhetoric. History's alienation from rhetoric—of which it had formerly been considered to be a branch, along with epistolography, philosophy, and romance (see Hugh Blair)—occurred at precisely the same time that literature or more accurately "literary writing" was being detached and differentiated from rhetorics. "Literature" was differentiated from rhetoric by Flaubert and others by the elevation of style conceived as the fusion in writing of perception and judgment over what had been taken to be the formulaic modes of expression of classical oratory on the one hand, and the relatively chaotic or "spontaneous" outpourings of Romantic "genius" on the other.

But—as Erich Auerbach and others have shown—the notion of "literature" elaborated over the course of the nineteenth century presumed a new "content" as well as new "forms." This content, formalized in the doctrine of "realism," was nothing other than what had come to be called "historical reality"—no longer limited to "the past" but extended to "the present" as well. If Auerbach is right, that "historism" which insisted on regarding every aspect of the past "in its own terms" and "for itself alone," without any impulse to generalize or judge it by transtemporal values or criteria, this historistic attitude is what informs and provides the ideology of literary realism and constitutes the basis of the specific kind of *knowledge* which the (realist) novel is considered to be capable of providing to the new social classes appearing in the wake of the French and American Revolutions, the advent of capitalism, and the beginning of the great modern European empires.[4]

The modern novel has its origin in the early eighteenth century in the transformation of the romance into a range of "how to live" manuals directed at middle-class women left at home and seeking instruction on "what must be done" in order to fulfill duties to God, husband, family, and friends in the absence of class practices of the kind that gave meaning to their peasant and aristocratic counterparts.[5] The assumption of male control over the development of the novel in the late eighteenth century transformed the novel into, first, the bildungsroman, and then, the novel of career, work, and love of classical realism. Class differences, career choices, new modes of work and labor, new sensibilities, indeed even new bodies (the unmarried uncle, the maiden aunt, the effete son, the promiscuous daughter)[6] suddenly appeared on the scene of "the historical present," and the realist novel, by the time it had taken the form and content given it by Balzac, Flaubert, Dickens, Jane Austen, George Eliot, Thackeray, and others, embarked upon that mapping of the new "historical reality" which taught four generations how to conjure with that "past in the present" that Joseph Conrad, Henry James, Oscar Wilde, Thomas Hardy, and Émile Zola would confront as an enigma which professional historical learning could not solve because it had become limited to dealing with "the facts" of the past. Small wonder that the next generation would, like Walter Benjamin, view professional historical learning as itself the impediment to any effort to probe the past of myth, memory, and dream as a resource for social and cultural renewal. History had gone from being a resource to being the problem itself. (Not of course for professional historians or most philosophers of history, but most certainly for writers, poets, and dramatists.)[7] Auerbach was surely right when he identified the content (or ultimate referent) of the modern realist novel as "historical reality" but it was "the practical past" rather than the "historical past" that the great novelists of the era were bringing to life.

Critical reflexivity can be directed at many different aspects of a writing practice as ancient and as venerable as historiography. One of the most important aspects of any scholarly practice that should be subjected to criticism and self-criticism is that congeries of presuppositions and assumptions which "go without saying," so obvious are they taken to be as foundational to the practice in question. In historical studies the distinction between fact and fiction is one such topos. It is this distinction which, in modern historical studies, presides over the opposition presumed to exist as a truth beyond question—namely, that history and literature are in some way so radically opposed to one another that any mixture of them must undermine the authority of the one and the value of the other.

And yet: the kind of storytelling which would subsequently come to be called "history" arose within the kinds of cultural practices which would subsequently come to be called "literature." And even though history has tried over the course of the last two centuries to become "scientific" and purge itself of the taint of its origins in "literature" (and more specifically, rhetoric), it has never fully succeeded in this endeavor. As the quotation from de Certeau which I have chosen as the epigraph of this chapter suggests, history has been unable to articulate its claim to scientificity without invoking "literature" as its antithetical other. It is this opposition of history to literature that sustains the belief, crippling to history's aspiration to serve as a "practical" discipline, that the imagination has no place in historical research, thinking, or writing about the past.

Recall that since its inception with Herodotus and Thucydides, history had been conceived as a pedagogical and indeed practical discipline par excellence.[8] As Foucault has reminded us, history has always—until relatively recently—functioned more as a practical, which is to say, an *ethical* discourse, rather than as a science. In ancient, modern, and even medieval times, historical discourse was recognized as a branch of rhetoric, itself second only to theology as the site of the ethical question: what is to be done? But as de Certeau insisted, the transformation of historical studies into a (pseudo-) science entailed its surrender of its authority to "teach philosophy by example" and provide credible exemplars of those attributes deemed necessary to and hence admirable by society.

True, its literary aspects were conceived to consist in the rhetorical and poetic embellishments by which hard truths and onerous duties were made palatable by mythification. Both Cicero and Saint Augustine allowed the use of what we might call literary fictions in the service of truth telling, which justified the post-Reformation belief in the possibility of distinguishing between good or morally responsible fictions on the one side and a sinful and degrading kind,on the other. With the transformation of history into a science, however, fiction in general and literary fiction in particular came to be viewed as the nefarious "other" of history and the kinds of truths about the past in which it dealt. Indeed, in Ranke and his progeny, the newly named category of "literature" (which included such genres as romance and the whole of rhetoric) was made to serve as history's negative, so that, by the late twentieth century, in the field of history, history writing with distinct literary features was immediately recognizable as the work of amateurs or, at best, as the product of a historical sensibility fallen prey to the lures of fantasy.

Now, at the same time that history was morphing into a (pseudo-) science, literature in general and the novel in particular were undergoing that revolution which would subsequently be labeled "realist." Realism has taken many different forms, but modern literary realism differs from others by (what Auerbach calls) a "historist" frame of mind, and more specifically by the extent to which writers such as Scott, Manzoni, Dumas, Stendhal, Balzac, Dickens, and Flaubert sought (quite in contrast to their professional historian counterparts) to represent "the present *as* history." As Auerbach notes, this effort to represent the present as history had to appear anomalous, because according to the doxa taking shape in professional historiography, historical knowledge was and could only be about the past.[9] Knowledge of the past could not be generalized and extended to the understanding of present circumstances, much less those of the future, without lapsing into ideological distortion and error. Thus, the novelists such as Balzac and Flaubert and Dickens who viewed the present as both a consequence and a fulfillment of the historical past and, at the same time, as undergoing changes caused by the very processes that had produced the past, violated the taboo of crossing the gap that separated the past from the present and allowed the present to be experienced as a stable platform from which the turmoil and conflict of the past could be contemplated *sine ira et studio*, as from a quiet and stable shore after a long passage at sea. The treatment of the present as history in realist literature effectively divided up the temporal continuum between historists and presentists, with the former consigned the task of mapping out the past in all its contingency and particularity and the latter assuming the role of "historicist" analysts of the new social reality emerging from the recent past of Revolution and Reaction. Indeed, the realist novel became the site where a newly legitimated dominant class could rehearse its role in the drama of desire's conflict with necessities which past generations had never dreamed of. Ironically, the more that history actually succeeded in transforming itself into a (kind of) science, objectivist, empiricist, particularist, the more remote the knowledge of the past which it produced became for generations confronting new social realities. And with the demystification of the world of the bourgeoisie effected by Marx, Darwin, and Freud, "history" alone remained as that reserve of fact and reality on which to base an idea of the present and a vision of a possible future. Whence the flourishing of what professional historians would contemn as "philosophy of history," born of the effort to generalize and synthesize the particular truths turned up by professional historians in their plundering of the archives of old Europe.

It is seldom noticed that growing up alongside of and mirroring the same drives that impelled to the creation of "philosophy of history" (Comte, Hegel, Buckle, Marx, Spencer, Taine, on to Spengler, Toynbee, T. Lessing, Vögelin, Croce, Gentile, and the rest) was another and more authoritative idea of what history and a temporality parsed by historical categories consisted of. This other idea of history erected alongside of and against the history of the historians flourished in literature, poetry, and drama, to be sure, but also and especially in the realist novel. And it resulted over time in the creation of a past quite different from that which served as the object of interest of professional historians. This was "the practical past" of my title, a past which, unlike that of the historians, has been lived by all of us more or less individually and more or less collectively and which serves as the basis for the kinds of perceptions of situations, solutions of problems, and judgments of value and worth that we must make in everyday situations of the kind never experienced by the "heroes" of history.

The distinction between "the historical past" and "the practical past" is useful for distinguishing between modern professional historians' approaches to the study of the past and the ways in which lay persons and practitioners of other disciplines call upon, recall, or seek to use "the past" as a "space of experience"[10] to be drawn upon as a basis for all kinds of judgments and decisions in daily life. The political, legal, and religious pasts can seldom be approached except by way of ideology or parti pris of some kind. These kinds of past can be said to belong to "history," no doubt about it, but they are seldom amenable to professional historians' techniques of investigation. Since such pasts are invested less in the interest of establishing the facts of a given matter than that of providing a basis in fact from which to launch a judgment of action in the present, they themselves cannot be handled according to the principle of "first the facts, then the interpretation" so dear to the professional historian's heart. For in inquiries into these kinds of past, what is at issue is not so much "What are the facts?" as, rather, "What will be allowed to count as a fact?" and, beyond that, "What will be permitted to pass for a specifically 'historical' as against a merely 'natural' (or for that matter, a 'supernatural') event?"

Now, it must be stressed that these two kinds of past are rather more ideal typifications than descriptions of actual points of view or ideologies. Moreover, it must be noted that professional historiography was set up (in the early nineteenth century) in the universities to serve the interests of the nation-state, to help in the work of creating national identities, and was used in the training of educators, politicians, colonial administrators, and both political and religious ideologues in manifestly "practical" ways. The famous "history as philosophy teaching by examples" or *historia magistra vitae* of nineteenth-century European culture was the same history that professional historians brokered as a past studied for itself alone and in its own terms, *sine ira et studio*. But this seeming duplicitousness on the part of professional historians was fully consonant with the contemporary ideology of science, which viewed the natural sciences as nothing if not both "disinterested" and "practical" or socially beneficial at one and the same time. Such a view of science was consistent with the reigning philosophies of positivism and utilitarianism which contributed to the transformation of a scientific world view into a whole Weltanschauung, which allowed "history" in general to be conceived as offering unimpeachable proof of the progress of civilization and the triumph of the white races of the world.

Of course, over the arc of the twentieth century, this myth of progress and the social Darwinism that sustained it were submitted to devastating critique. To which professional historiography responded by retreating into a kind of commonsensical empiricism as justification for the neutrality and disinterestedness with which it composed its ideologically anodyne pictures of the historical past. This empiricism allowed professional historiography to continue to trumpet its ideological neutrality ("just the facts, and nothing but the facts") while disdaining "philosophy of history" of the kind inherited from Comte, Hegel, and Marx and promoted by Spengler, Toynbee, and Croce over the span of the two World Wars as mere "ideology" or as religious prophecy masquerading as "historical science." (See, for example, Popper and Collingwood.)

Now, philosophy of history—however prophetic, predictive, or apocalyptic it may be—was not in general intended as an alternative to what is called "straight history." Most philosophers of history—from Hegel on—regarded their work as an extension of or supplement to the work of ordinary historians. They saw themselves as providing procedures for summarizing, synthesizing, or symbolizing the myriads of works written by working historians in order to derive some general principles regarding the nature of human beings' existence with others in time. Whether they did this adequately or not is a moot point. Because whether philosophers of history have used the knowledge and information cooked up by ordinary historians well or badly is not a matter for historians to decide—any more than it is a matter for physicists to decide how the knowledge they produce may be put to use by engineers, inventors, entrepreneurs, or for that matter military establishments. Surely there is no difference between a philosopher's ruminations on the nature of art based on his considerations of specific art objects and the work of historians of art and the use of historians' works to try to divine not so much the meaning *in* history as, rather, the kinds of meanings that can be derived from the study of historians' writings.

In any event, I do not wish to follow this line of discussion because, as history shows us, genuine historians are chary of philosophy of history for their own good reasons, and there seems to be little chance of bringing them onto common ground in the foreseeable future. But it has to be said that, whatever else it may be, philosophy of history belongs to the class of disciplines meant to bring order and reason to a "practical past" rather than to that "historical past" constructed by professional historians for the edification of their peers in their various fields of study.

But this differentiation between the past constructed by historians and that constructed by philosophers of history permits insight, or so it seems to be, into a relationship that has been particularly worrisome in modern Western scientific culture—namely, the relationship between fact and fiction (sometimes referred to as that between history and literature) within the context of cultural modernism.

In the many discussions of postmodernism that have taken place since Lyotard's famous essay on the topic,[11] few people have thought it important to notice that the dominant genre and mode of postmodernist writing is the (neo) historical novel.[12] To be sure, mainstream critics lamented what was taken to be an unfortunate (not to say disastrous) mixture (or scumbling) of the distinction between fact and fiction or reality and fantasy, for it seemed to violate a taboo that had sustained the possibility of a certain kind of "serious" fiction writing, by which I mean a kind of (modernist) which took the relation between past and present (or memory and perception) as its principal object of interest. I refer to the work of the first generation of modernist writers as represented by Conrad, Proust, Joyce, Eliot, Pound, Woolf, Kafka, Stein, Gide, and others, all of whom seemed to turn against "history" as a cause rather than a solution to the problem of how to deal with a present oppressed by the remains of the past.

Literary modernism has been charged in recent years with a kind of narcissistic "presentism," with a defective sense of history, a retreat into irrationalism and psychosis, a disdain for the truth of fact, and a return to what T. S. Eliot, in his review of Joyce's *Ulysses*, praised as "the mythic method." But the revival in the second half of the twentieth century of the early nineteenth-century genre of the historical novel (Scott, Manzoni, Dumas, Balzac) raises questions about its ideological significance. Moreover, the fact that it is the *historical* novel rather than any of the other genres (epistolary, Gothic, bildungsroman, realist) that might have been revived raises questions about the status of that "history" which is used to indicate the *kind* of novel which the postmodernists have chosen for the presentation of life "in modern times." In other words, in choosing the genre of the "historical novel," postmodernist writers as different as Pynchon, Mailer, Capote, DeLillo, Roth, Pat Barker, W. G. Sebald, Coetzee, Grass, Danilo Kiš, Robert Rosenstone, William Gass, and any number of others challenged the dogma which made of "historical facts" the standard by which to assess the realism of *any* discourse about the real past or present.

Recall that the archetypal historical novel, Sir Walter Scott's *Waverley or 'Tis Sixty Years Since* (1805, published 1814), apologetically violated the taboo on mixing historical fact with fantasy or romance in his account of the adventures of a "normal" young man who enters into the service of George II of England, is sent to the Highlands of Scotland, and finds passion, love, adventure, and indeed commits treason and murder before being returned to the fold of a social order that will emerge from the Napoleonic Wars with a new ruling elite and worldwide empire. The novel openly asks the question as to what had been gained and lost to the British people by the transition to modernity, as represented by the suppression of the Jacobite Rebellion of 1745. Edward Waverley is, as it were, run through a number of tests and put over a number of hurdles and in the process allows Scott to explicate the virtues and vices of the older culture of the Scottish or Highlands clans and assess the weaknesses and strengths of the emergent social order. Over the course of the nineteenth century, the novel was condemned for mixing fact and fancy in such a way as to endow them with the same tincture or color. This was bad enough—in a moral sense—but beyond this Scott consciously violated what would soon become an element of orthodoxy in the emergent ideology of historism: the use of anachronism. Young Edward Waverley has the *forma mentis* of a young gentleman of Scott's own time, rather than that of a young gentleman of modest means of the mid-eighteenth century, while every other figure in the novel is given the aura or mystique of Highlands culture of long ago. This technique of anachronism continued to be used down to the late nineteenth century to dramatize what Georg Lukács called the "dialectical relation" and what Benjamin would take to be the "dialectical image" of a time and place undergoing profound changes of a specifically historical kind. Although the book and the genre of the historical novel were a great success. the mixture of fact and fiction was condemned not only by historians but by moralists in general.[13] The mixture of fact and fiction was regarded as not only mistaken but morally offensive.

At the same time, of course, the profession of historical studies was finding its own new orthodoxy and becoming transformed into the official custodian of "the past," but a past which differed from the past of both memory and fantasy, a past which would come to be called "the historical past." The use of the term "historical" as a modifier of the substantive "past" indicates an exclusion and a condensation: an exclusion of any other past from the "historical" and a condensation of the past as *only* historical. From now on, the past of nature, of animality, and of humanity, even the pasts of all those "histories" which existed before the invention of "History," will be shunted aside and measured, for their truth and their reality, against the pure past of "history." The idea of a specifically historical past, different from the rest of the past, the past not authenticated by "historical learning," is the substance of the idea of historism (*Historismus*). In the mapping of this past, the imagination has no part (see Hobsbawm).

Once I had the temerity to suggest that historical writing was not so much *opposed* to literary writing as rather related to it in the manner of what Wittgenstein called a family resemblance. After all, traditional historical writing (cast in the mode and genre of the narrative) *manifestly* resembled such genres of fiction as the epic, the romance, the comedy, the tragedy, and indeed myth in general. And insofar as the form (or container) of an utterance had to be considered as an element of its content (referent or substance), then the genre of the history could claim no exemption from the charge of fictionalizing any more than a fairy tale could do.

Of course, anyone who thought that the form and the content of a discourse could be dissociated and each criticized on its own terms without significant loss of meaning would not buy this argument. Especially those who had a disciplinary investment in maintaining the *essential* difference—to the point of an irresolvable opposition—between fact and fiction. It offended common sense if not critical theory to suggest that while the main content of a historical discourse might very well be "facts," its form was the stuff of fiction and that, therefore, its overall message inevitably consisted of a mixture of fact and fiction.

The metafiction of the historical narrative consisted of something like this: Here is a congeries of facts organized for presentation as if they were (or had the form of) a literary and more specifically a fictional thing. The form of the story is just there to make the information (facts and arguments about the facts, their nature, relationships, etc.) more palatable. So read and enjoy but once you are done, kick away the fictional ladder on which you have climbed and contemplate the facts in themselves for what they tell you about a "form of life" now dead and past.

Now, obviously, the separation of fact and fiction in the act of reading a discourse of any kind is not so easy. Indeed, as almost everyone would grant, the story form imports particular kinds of valorization, most especially of an emotive or affectual kind, into the account of whatever has been posited as the referent. The same set of events can be emplotted as a tragedy or as a romance with a shift of point of view or perspective (i.e., mode), and it matters whether a given set of events is presented in a voice that is ironic or sentimental or reverent, and so on. Indeed, even diction (word choice) and the tropes of grammar tincture the presentation and tilt reception in different directions. Everyone knows this, but it is hard to swallow if you are committed to telling the truth, the whole truth, and nothing but the truth in what you say.

Of course, I now recognize that I made a mistake by once suggesting that the problem consisted of the relationship between two *substances*, "fact" on the one hand, "fiction" on the other. I might well have said that the problem had to do with a discourse (history) that wished to be faithful to its referent but which had inherited conventions of representation that produced meaning in excess of what it literally asserted of a kind that were identifiably literary if not fictionalizing in their effects. I hasten to add that I am not prepared to extend this idea beyond the domain of historical discourse which typically has to do with referents that are past and hence no longer open to empirical inspection. And it would not be very important if historical discourse had not quietly slipped into the place formerly occupied by religion and metaphysics and become a kind of degree zero of factuality on which the other human and social sciences could draw as a fund of what Foucault calls "empiricities" for the kinds of operations they want to carry out in the creation of their lore about what human being might be. History has fulfilled an important social role in limiting itself to establishing what really happened in discrete domains of the past and resisting any impulse to draw lessons for the present or, God forbid, daring to predict what lies in store for us in the future. But history reads us moral lessons, whether we would have it or not, simply by virtue of the casting of its accounts of the past in the form of stories. More generally, it performs this operation simply by its use of natural language to describe its objects of interest and report the historian's thoughts about what these objects really are, what they did or what happened to them, and how they came to assume the shapes they have assumed in the discourses we write about them. This is because natural languages come laden with a cargo of connotation over which writers and speakers have no control and which scatters meaning over referents quite as randomly as Jackson Pollock spattered buckets of paint over a canvas from atop his stepladder. And this is as true of historical documents as it is of a historian's own prose.

But what does all this imply for our understanding of history's place in contemporary human sciences?

First, it allows us to comprehend the continued interest in speculative philosophy of history, of the Hegel-Marx kind, in spite of the fact that both professional historians and many philosophers have consistently denied its legitimacy. Many assume that speculative philosophy of history is a secular form of religious apocalypticism, metaphysics, or myth. And yet, if it is any or all of these things, this suggests that speculative philosophy of history is motivated by the same kind of practical concerns that motivate those modernist and postmodernist novelists to take as their primary referent what they think of as "history" but which is actually "the practical past." I for one have never bought Jean-François Lyotard's idea that the essence of postmodernism is to be found in the repudiation of *les grands récits* of metahistory. It may be true that philosophers have ruled speculative philosophy of history out of court, but this is not true of art in general or of the modernist and postmodernist novel in particular. Because the modern novel and its modernist counterpart have been interested in history for the same reasons that speculative philosophy of history has been interested in it: for practical reasons. Thus, while I argued in *Metahistory* that every work of historiography presupposes a whole philosophy of history, so too I would argue now that every *modern* novel presupposes a philosophy of history. Consider the following case.

Toni Morrison's masterpiece, *Beloved*, manifestly a meditation on the place of slavery in American culture and society and the implications thereof for an understanding of the role of African Americans in contemporary American society, is presented by the author in the fourth printing of the work as an exercise in the "philosophy of history." In her explanation of how she conceived the uses to be made of historical accounts of a young escaped slave woman, Margaret Garner, who had killed one of her children rather than have it returned to the condition of a slave in the South, Toni Morrison begins by describing her own situation as a black woman in a putatively "liberated" society of the 1980s:

> I think now it was the shock of liberation that drew my thoughts to what "free" could possibly mean to women. In the eighties, the debate was still roiling: equal pay, equal treatment, access to professions, schools . . . and choice without stigma. To marry or not. To have children or not.

> Inevitably these thoughts led me to *the different history of black women in this country*—a *history* in which marriage was discouraged, impossible, or illegal; in which birthing children was required, but having them, being responsible for them—being, in other words, their parent—was as out of the question as freedom. Assertions of parenthood under conditions peculiar to the logic of institutional enslavement were criminal.

Toni Morrison then recalls how, in an earlier time, her attention had been turned to the "historical" Margaret Garner, who had become a cause célèbre in the fight against the Fugitive Slave laws, which mandated the return of escapees to their owners. Her sanity and lack of repentance caught the attention of abolitionists as well as newspapers. She was certainly single-minded and, judging by her comments, she had the intellect, the ferocity, and the willingness to risk everything for what was to her the necessity of freedom.[14]

The question, for Morrison, at that time was how to use the facts of Margaret Garner's life for insight into the ethical issues with which a black woman in her situation and in her time had been confronted.[15] She proceeds to draw a distinction between the "historical Margaret Garner" and what I would wish to call the "poetical" Margaret Garner, by which I mean, the flesh-and-blood woman who was capable of the kind of tragic actions traditionally ascribed only to the archetypal figures of myth, religion, and art. Thus, Morrison writes: "The *historical Margaret Garner* is fascinating, but, to a novelist, too confining. Too little imaginative space there for my purposes." (emphasis mine)

I take this statement to mean that those aspects of Margaret Garner's story capable of illuminating and serving as a goad to ethically responsible action in the present could not be truthfully presented in a strictly historiological treatment. The kind of *documentation* required for this could not possibly be provided. So Morrison takes another route, that of invention:

> *So I would invent her thoughts*, plumb them for *a subtext that was historically true in essence, but not strictly factual* in order to relate her history to contemporary issues about freedom, responsibility, and women's "place." (emphases mine)

"A subtext that was historically true in essence, but not strictly factual . . ."—I would amend this to read: "a subtext that was true in its *historical essence* but not strictly factual." For how could an account of the "thoughts" of a real person in the past be both "historically true" and "not strictly factual"? And, more pertinently, what is or might be a "historical essence" of a person's "thoughts"?

Here we come to the real problem that confronts us in trying to theorize the relation between the historical past and its practical counterpart. For our interest in the practical past must take us beyond "the facts" as conventionally understood in historiological thinking. Indeed, it must take us beyond the idea that a fact, whatever else it may be, is identifiable by its logical opposition to "fiction," where fiction is understood to be an imaginary thing or product of the imagination. Would this mean that Toni Morrison, in inventing the thoughts of Margaret Garner, is effectively "fictionalizing" them?

Morrison glosses this statement thus: "The heroine would represent *the unapologetic acceptance of shame and terror; assume the consequences of choosing infanticide; claim her own freedom*." (emphasis mine) The historical Margaret Garner is to be turned into a "figure," a figure recognizable by the archetype of Medea, a heroine who *unapologetically accepts* the shame and terror of her deed, *assumes* the consequences of *choosing* infanticide, and thereby *claims* her own freedom. And although Morrison makes little of it, the fact is that there is nothing in this characterization of her heroine that is at odds with what is known about the "historical Margaret Garner." What kind of fiction—a fiction that is in no way at odds with the known facts—would that be?

Let us suppose that what we have here is a case in which the opposition of fact to fiction obscures more than it illuminates. I have argued elsewhere that, when it is a matter of dealing with those aspects of reality which force us to question the reality or even the possibility of our ideals of humanity—as in American slavery or the Holocaust—the writer interested in facing directly the ethical issues (the question: what should I do?) involved in the consideration of such phenomena might well take on the role of performing *in* writing the kind of action being presented as event. Which, in the case of Toni Morrison in this instance, is unapologetically accepting responsibility for inventing the thoughts of her protagonist, assuming the consequences of presuming to reconstruct a history that strains credibility, and, in so doing, claiming her freedom to deal with the past in a way consonant with her situation in her present. For, as she rightly indicates, the "terrain" of "slavery" is not only "formidable and pathless," but also "repellent," "hidden," and "deliberately buried" and—I would add—not least by historians who limit themselves to the recounting of the facts of the matter. This was, indeed, "to pitch a tent in a cemetery inhabited by highly vocal ghosts" who were accessible to the poetic imagination in ways that the historiographer can never be allowed to imagine.

CHAPTER 2

Truth and Circumstance

What (if Anything) Can Properly Be Said about the Holocaust?

Under what circumstances would it be impertinent, tactless, or simply irrelevant to ask of a discourse which manifestly refers to the real world, past, present, or future, the question: "Is it true?" And if there are certain utterances (expressions, allusions, suggestions, statements, propositions, or assertions) about the real world for which the question, "Is it true?" is beside the point, what kinds of responses, if any, would be appropriate for utterances of this kind?

I pose these questions in the context of an ongoing discussion of what would constitute a "proper" representation of the Holocaust, an event so traumatic for so many individuals and groups that, when irrefutable evidence of its occurrence became public, incredulity was the first and most dominant response to it. Even after incredulity gave way to outrage over the fact that a "modern," "enlightened," "Christian," and "humanistic" nation like Germany could betray the values of the European civilization of which it had been an esteemed representative, the question of what the Final Solution amounted to, what it signified about European values themselves, what it told one about modernity, Germany, "the Jews" and Judaism, and "Europe" in general remained pressing and seemingly intractable. For historians—professional custodians of Western historical consciousness and cultivators of a putative science of history—the principal question raised by the Holocaust was its identity as a specifically "historical" event and the best way to inscribe it within, insert it into, assimilate it to the normative narrative account of Europe's history. At the same time, the sense that the Holocaust was an "unusual," "novel," and possibly even a "unique" event in Europe's history raised the possibility of having to revise this history radically in order to do justice to the insights into the *real* nature of European civilization which the event had seemingly provided. In fact, the "extremity" if not the uniqueness of the Holocaust event raised crucial questions about the theoretical presuppositions underlying and informing modern Western ideas about "history," the methodologies utilized by modern professional historians in their efforts to know the historical past, and the protocols and techniques used for the presentation of historical reality in their discourses.

These questions were rendered more difficult to answer due to the fact that modern media had made possible the recording and circulation of so many personal accounts of survivors' experiences of the event and, moreover, the demand on the part of many of these "witnesses" to the event that their remembered experiences be factored into the "official" or "doxological" record being built up by the historians on the basis of their examination of the documentary and monumentary evidence available to them. Beyond that, while the historians' reconstruction of what had really happened in the Final Solution and/or the Holocaust was proceeding at a customarily glacial pace, the field of Holocaust studies was being flooded by a plethora of memoirs, autobiographies, novels, plays, movies, poems, and documentaries, which, from the standpoint of many historians, threatened to aestheticize, fictionalize, kitschify, relativize, and otherwise mythify what was an undeniable fact (or congeries of facts) and as such "properly" studied only by means and methods more or less scientific. This meant that, from the standpoint of many historians, when presented with any representation of the Final Solution or the Holocaust, the first and most basic question had to be: "Is it true?" And if the answer to that question was either no or contained some equivocation, then the representation in question had to be rejected as being not only a misrepresentation of reality but, given the nature of the hurt visited upon the victims, a violation of victims' moral right to a true and accurate account of what they had experienced.

But what about that vast mass of testimony of survivors? Should it, too, be submitted to the same criterion of truthfulness as that demanded of a historian's account of some event in the past? We must undoubtedly demand that the person bearing witness to some experience at least wishes to tell the truth, but is a correspondence model of truth our principal interest in the testimony of survivors? Obviously, it must be our primary concern if the testimony is offered in a court of law where the determination of what happened and who was responsible for it are our principal interests. But when it is a matter of giving voice to what it felt like to be subjected to the kind of treatment that the victims of the Holocaust experienced, a correspondence ideal of truthfulness would seem to be an improper demand. Even the coherence model of truthfulness would seem to have little relevance in the assessment of the authority of the testimony of a victim. Here the question, "is it true?" should only be posed as a "rhetorical" one.

I will return to the status of victims' testimony later on. For the moment, I want to extend the investigation of the pertinence of the question, "Is it true?" to the consideration of artistic and specifically literary treatments of the Holocaust. Of course, artistic and literary treatments of the Holocaust must be a problem for historians of the Holocaust who regard this event as having something like a sacral status. And this is especially the case when "artistic" is identified with "aesthetic" and "literature" is identified with "fiction." It is the necessity of these two sets of identifications that I wish to question.

If the Holocaust is conceded an ontological status that would prohibit its representation in images or as an occasion for anything other than reverence or celebration, then obviously any artistic or literary treatment of the Holocaust would have to be viewed as approaching near to the status of blasphemy. This attitude would rule out in advance any historiographical treatment of the Holocaust insofar as it might use aestheticizing or fictionalizing strategies in the composition of the presentation. And yet, in my view at least, this is exactly what a narratological treatment of the Holocaust or any part of it would do. This is why, for example, the philosopher (and my dear friend) Berel Lang counsels the abandonment of any attempt to narrativize the Holocaust and suggests instead that accounts remain at the level of a chronicle, a simple listing of the facts in the order of their occurrence as established by a literalist reading of the documentary record.

Berel Lang is quite right to view narrative or narrativization or, more simply, storytelling as less a veridical mimesis of a course of real events than a "dangerous supplement" to a rigorously truthful account of them.[1] For Berel Lang, the making of a story out of the events of the Holocaust is another instance of figuration which sacrifices any possibility of a literal account of it to the exigencies of aesthetic fancy or play. An aesthetic treatment of the Holocaust, in his view, subordinates the truth of fact to the egoistic display of the artist's technique or the ambiguating effects of rhetorical or poetic figuration. In this view, Berel Lang joins forces with Carlo Ginzburg's efforts to defend the historian's truth from the corroding effects of skepticism and relativism. Ginzburg objects to relativism because it eschews the possibility of a single correct view of the world and to skepticism because—in his view—it forecloses the very possibility of truth itself. Pluralism and skepticism together license an "anything goes" attitude toward truth and an "any given view is as valid as any other" attitude toward values.[2] Lang provides arguments against aestheticism and fictionalism in the treatment of any event with the moral weight and ontological substance of the Holocaust.

Now, in my contribution to the conference on "The Final Solution and the Limits of Representation," organized by Saul Friedländer and Wulf Kansteiner at UCLA in 1990, I took the position that the problem of representing the Holocaust should not be conceptualized in terms of traditional (late nineteenth century) notions of realism, history, representation, aesthetics, fiction, ideology, discourse, storytelling, and mimeticist notions of description. The idea was that, as the occurrence of the Holocaust itself had made obvious, the combination of the new reality manifested in World War II and the consolidation of modernist notions of the nature of discourse, representation, history, and art itself had rendered questionable if not nugatory the pre–World War II notions of these issues.

I do not wish to rehearse once more my attempts to formulate these issues as I did then. What I want to do, rather, is try to confront the issue of how to present the Holocaust as a historical phenomenon, the "novelty" not to say the "anomalous" nature of which in modern European history I willingly concede, by a consideration of the stakes that are involved in the posing of the question, "Is it true?" when confronted with any and every instance of Holocaust representation, in historiography, in literature, in film, in photography, in philosophy, in social science, and so on.

And this assessment extends to the manifestly artistic versions of victims' testimony, to memoirs such as Primo Levi's *Se questo è un uomo* (*If This Is a Man*), to comix like Art Spiegelman's *Maus*, and films like Cavani's *Il portiere di notte* (*The Night Porter*), Spielberg's *Schindler's List*, and Benigni's *La vita è bella* (*Life Is Beautiful*). Although all of these artistic works are manifestly *about* the real historical event, the Holocaust, they are viewed by many historians as not only "unhistorical" but as "fictionalizing" or "aestheticizing" of an event which, by its nature, has a moral right to a strictly truthful account of its reality.[3]

And it is here that I wish to question the pertinence, aptness, tactfulness, and adequacy of the question, "Is it true?" to *all* discourses making reference to real historical events in the course of their elaboration. My answer to this question will be something like, yes, it is always pertinent to raise the question, "Is it true?" of any account of the past presenting itself as a *historical* account thereof. But, I will suggest, this question, "Is it true?" is of secondary importance to discourses making reference to the real world (past or present) cast in a mode other than that of simple declaration. This is especially the case with artistic (verbal, aural, or visual) representations of reality (past or present) which, in modernity, are typically cast in modes other than that of simple declaration—for example, the interrogative, imperative, and subjunctive modes.[4]

The question I have posed, "When is the question, 'Is it true?' irrelevant?" is often discussed in terms of the morality of truth telling; for example, when is it proper or desirable to tell a lie or, put another way, do circumstances make it "better" to tell a lie rather than the truth? This question does not interest me. I am interested in the question, is it proper to forgo asking the question, "Is it true or false?" in the presence of a specific kind of discourse of which witness literature would be a paradigm and a modernist literary treatment of the Holocaust would be an instance.[5] This question interests me because of a belief amongst some historians that a history and all of the statements made about history or the past must "tell the truth." Moreover, it is a principle of historiographical statements that they must not "lie," "distort," or "misrepresent," or deny, leave out, negate, or disavow those "facts" which have been established with regard to some aspect of past "reality." All of this is bad enough, according to the moral epistemology that informs much of current thought about historical writing—it is much, much worse to "fictionalize" history either in the sense of presenting "fictional" things as "facts," the sense of turning "facts" into fictions, or mixing facts with fiction as in the nefarious historical novel or historical movie or the so-called "docudrama" (which is supposed to be a "dramatization" of some historical reality). This crime, sin, or misdemeanor is deemed to be akin to the feared "mythification" of reality or "metahistorical" treatment of historical reality after the manner of Hegel, Marx, Nietzsche, Spengler, Toynbee, and so on.

Now, in my opinion Holocaust "discourse" is not only about the kinds of questions I have listed above, it also includes the actual histories or historical treatments of the Holocaust insofar as they present or perform certain answers to theoretical questions in the course of their attempts to provide answers to a set of purely "factual" questions. And this is so from the moment when the question, "What is it?" is posed all the way over to the time when, in the book or article actually published, one can see manifested the statement, "This is what happened." The *theoretical* question, "What is it I see before me?" belongs to the same discourse as the answer cast in the mode of a set of facts which add up to the statement: "What you see before you is a Holocaust, genocide, extermination, and other such crimes." And because the theoretical question, "What is it?" belongs to the same discourse as the answer, "It is an X," we cannot legitimately (i.e., with a logic that is not tautological) point to any given history of the Holocaust written by any given historian as an *example* of a "proper" treatment of it.

What is proper to anything is both a question of fact (what does it look like or what are its attributes? what did it do?) and a question of morality (what is its "nature," its "essence," its "substance" in reference to which alone one might determine the "propriety" which is to say, the "self-sameness" of a thing's motion, movement, desire, judgment, action, etc.). *Authenticity* (the circumstance in which a thing *appears to be* exactly what it is or always *is* what it appears to be) might also be defined as doing the proper thing, at the proper time, and in the proper place, with the proper aim, object, and goal in mind and the proper means for doing just that thing and not something else. The difficulty of living up to this ideal of authenticity is manifest in situations in which it is the "nature" of the thing that is being assessed as to its authenticity or self-sameness that is at issue.

Thus, if in support of a particular notion of what the Holocaust is or might be or must be taken to have been, I bring out a specific representation of it as an example of what an authentic or proper presentation of it is to be taken to be, my judgment of it has to be taken to be either assertoric, categorical, or problematical, which is to say, either in the mode of a hypothesis, in the mode of an imperative, or in the mode of a question. If *assertoric*, then the example can be considered for use as a model generating hypotheses to be tested out in the manner of an interrogation. If *categorical*, then the example is to be taken as a paradigm or original instance that will not only suggest to us what kinds of questions are properly posed to the thing being interrogated, but also the moral stance proper to the inquiry. Whereas a *problematical* example features aporia, or the difficulty of deciding whether the proper is to be considered an assertoric or a categorical instance. Here I follow the Kant of *Groundwork of the Metaphysics of Morals*.[6]

Kant thought that in any inquiry into an ethical matter, we could not legitimately use an example to suggest the principle being sought by which to guide inquiry "properly," because the principle in question had to be sought in the operations of a reason purged of both moral and aesthetic "interests." But if the issue in question is the proper, which is a moral question, pure (or scientific) reason cannot provide what we are looking for in seeking the rule of "propriety" in the first place. If in making a statement of what one *ought* to do in trying to compose a representation of an event like the Holocaust with proper concern for its real "nature," I advance an argument giving my reasons for recommending one mode of approaching the phenomenon over another, my statement has to be taken as a kind of recommendation or an imperative. Here is an example: "Consider this way of treating the history of the Holocaust (that of, for example, Christopher Browning rather than that of Daniel Goldhagen)" or, alternatively, "Write the history of the Holocaust in this way and no other!"

Now, in neither case is "Is it true?" a proper response to utterances of the kind, "Consider this!" or "Do this!" Is it true that I ought to consider writing my history of the Holocaust on the model of X? Or alternatively: Is it true that I must write the history of the Holocaust, not only in a given manner but also cast in a particular mode (by which I mean a specific attitude of submission, reverence, or care vis à vis the object of study)? For the question, "Is it true that I *ought* to do P?" is a deontological question, which is to say, a matter of obligation, and one proper response to it is to ask either: "Says who?" or "To what or whom am I obligated to do P?" And if the answer to this question is something like, you are obligated by the very nature of the event of which you are writing a history, you can see that we are back to the original question: What is the nature of this event called the Holocaust?

The difficulty in which much of Holocaust discourse has become mired is that the telling of the truth about anything can come modalized in ways other than an answer to the simple declarative sentence which is usually taken by philosophers to be the model of statements claiming to be true. To be sure, statements of the kind, "It is the case that (or it is true that) snow is white or the cat is on the mat" are properly responded to by the question, "Is it true that . . . ?" But statements cast in the form of questions ("Where is the cat?"), desires ("Would that I had a cat"), even imperatives ("Find the cat!") are hardly answerable by the question: "Is it true?"

All this is elementary, to be sure. But if we extend the idea of modality from sentences to whole discourses, we can even entertain the idea that whole novels, dramas, histories, and (who knows?) even philosophical discourses might be cast in a variety of modes that deprives even their factual statements of the force of declaratives. Limiting my remarks now to my own area of interest and the hypothesis that there is more than one way to "tell the truth about the past," I wish to suggest that both the historical novel and the novelesque history are instances of nondeclarative discourses, that their truth may consist less in what they *assert* in the mode of factual truth telling than in what they *connote* in the other moods and voices identified in the study of grammar: which is to say, the *modes* of interrogation, conation or coaction, and subjunction and the *voices* of action, passion, and transumption. Thus, for example, it might make less sense to respond to a poem or a novel or a history cast in the mode of a question or a wish with the query, "Is it true?" than it does to respond to one cast in the mode of a command. The "proper" response to a command might be, "Yes, sir" or "No, sir" but it is not necessarily (in the case in which a command is uttered outside a military or a master-slave relation) improper to respond, as in the case with Melville's "Bartleby the Scrivener," with the subjunctive statement "I would prefer not."

Considerations such as these move us over into the domain of speech act theory, in which propriety of response to an utterance is "context specific" and "conditions of felicity" (which is to say, propriety) may apply. In the case of research into the past, there are a number of different ways of addressing, observing, hailing, or otherwise investing the past. Thus, for example, one might approach the past as a place from which one or one's group has descended. Or (quite a different matter) one might regard the past as a place of one's origin. Again, one might take up a position vis à vis the past as what has already happened or what has been done or what has been made before one had appeared on the scene. This sense of the past as that which has already been done might in turn be taken up as either a heritage or as a burden to be cast off and, in either case, a presence *which seems to present itself* (apodictically) either as an enigma (a puzzle waiting to be solved, as in Pynchon's *Crying of Lot 49*) or as an anomaly (a real problem for which there may be no solution, as in Toni Morrison's *Beloved*).

I would like to recall that speech act theory was intended, according to J. L. Austin, its founder, to undermine ("play old Harry with") two fetishisms: the "true/false fetish" and the "value/fact fetish."[7] According to Austin, the crucial instance of speech act theory is to be found in the class of speech acts he calls "behabitives," which is to say, such behaviors as "apologizing," "congratulating," "commanding," "consoling," "cursing," and "challenging."[8]

Behabitives belong, according to Austin, to one of five classes of speech acts which also include: verdictives (giving a verdict, appraising), exercitives (appointing, voting, ordering), commissives (promising, announcing, espousing), and expositives (arguing, conversing, illustrating, exemplifying). Austin goes on to say that he finds the last two classes of speech acts, that is, expositives and behabitives, "most troublesome: behabitives . . . because they seem too miscellaneous altogether; and expositives because they are enormously numerous and important, and seem both to be included in the other classes and at the same time to be unique in a way that I have not succeeded in making clear even to myself. It could well be said that all aspects are present in all my classes . . ." In other words, by Austin's own account, his effort to define or identify the essence of speech acts is problematic: his discourse is expositive but leaves open the ethical (or behabitive) question: given this exposition of the phenomenon called speech acts, what should I do?

So, supposing I am a historian, interested as I am in the history of modern Germany, the history of Jewish communities in modern Europe, the "places" of the Final Solution, the Holocaust, the genocide, the extermination, and so forth, in these histories, the meaning of this event for the understanding of what was really happening in the times and places of these histories. And because I am aware of the "special" or "extreme" or "exceptional" nature of this event—its embarrassment not only to Europeans but to many other groups to their own amour propre and the *threat* that this event poses to their sense of their own individual and group identity—supposing that I know that this event has a significance that is not only factualistic (in the sense that it happened where and when and how it did) but also ethical, insofar as it manifests the violation of a fundamental principle of our humanity: namely, that thou shalt not treat another human being as less than human, which is also the rule of modern humanistic historiological inquiry; and that thou shalt treat every human being in history as partaking in the *humanitas* which all humans share in. Given these suppositions, the question arises: does the evidence that comes to us from this event which we are studying in order to find out not only *that* it happened and *how* it happened, but also and more importantly, does it tell us what were the conditions of the possibility of its happening? Which, if we are to take Aristotle seriously (and how could we not?), puts the ball out of the court of both philosophy and history and into that of *poiesis*: "poetry" or literary art understood as a mode of cognition focused on the possible, rather than on the actual (history, as Aristotle understood it) and the universal (philosophy, as he understood it). Indeed, I would suggest at this point in my own discourse that the speech act theory of J. L. Austin (who was practical enough to have participated in the planning of the Normandy invasion) is or can legitimately be considered to be a theory of the poetic function of language (as against its referential, expressive, conative, phatic, and metalinguistic functions), for what else is poetic utterance but a doing or making of something by a particular mode, manner, or style of saying something?[9]

Recall now that for Austin a speech act is "illocutionary": that is, an action in which, in saying something, one not only *says* something but also *does* something; that is to say, changes a relationship either of the speaker to the world, of one part of the world to another, or of the world to the speaker. And if this is right—as many of Austin's commentators seem to think that it is right—then we might begin to think about discourses, of which "historiography" would be one, as speech acts which, in saying something about the world, seek to change the world, the way one might relate to it, or the way things relate to one another in the world. In other words, Austin's theory of speech acts might be used to contrive a discourse or a congeries of discourses such as "historiography" as a praxis, which is to say, an action intended to change or have an impact on the world by the *way* it says something about it. (I take it that such a principle underlies the belief in the right of courts to deem Holocaust denial a crime to be punished by a fine or incarceration or some other sanction. The Holocaust denier has not only said something, he has also *done* something in the saying; that is, he has changed or tried to change relationships in the real world in the way that a curse or magical spell is supposed to do. Which is why those historians who objected to the designation of Holocaust denial as a crime perceived aright what the courts had overlooked—namely, that if denial of a fact established by historians constitutes a crime, then the distinction between honest error and malicious error must go by the board. The proper response to someone who denies the Holocaust is not "Is it true?" but, rather the question, "What motivates the desire driving the denial?")

An example of a text, although manifestly *about* the real world and specifically the world of Auschwitz, to which a response cast in the form, "Is it (historically) true?" would be tactless, is Primo Levi's memoir of his time in Auschwitz in the late months of World War II. Obviously, Levi's *Se questo è un uomo*[10] contains a multitude of declarative utterances which ask to be taken as true in the literal sense of that term (that is, as referentially true and semantically meaningful). But the title of Levi's memoir is taken from the poem that serves as the epigraph of the work and as the paratextual paradigm of the work's intended meaning-effect. It begins with a title, "Shema," the Jewish declaration of faith in Israel, and an address, not to the prospective reader, but to an anonymous "you":

You who live secure
In your warm houses,
You who return at evening
To find warm food and friendly faces,
Consider if this is a man
Who works in mud
Who knows no peace
Who fights for a piece of bread
Who dies by a yes or a no
Consider if this is a woman,
Without hair or a name
Without strength to remember
With vacant eyes and a cold womb
Like a frog in winter
Meditate on these things
I charge you with these words.
Engrave them on your hearts
When at home or on the way
When you retire and when you rise.
Repeat them to your children
Or may your house crumble
Disease afflict you,
Your children turn their faces from you.

Voi che vivete sicuri
Nelle vostre tiepide case,
Voi che trovate tornando a sera

Il cibo caldo e visi amici:
Considerate se questo è un uomo
Che lavora nel fango
Che non conosce pace
Che lotta per mezzo pane
Che muore per un si o no.
Considerate se questo è una donna
Senza capelli e senza nome
Senza più forza di ricordare
Vuoti gli occhi e freddo il grembo
Come un rana d'inverno
Meditate che questo è stato:
Vi commando queste parole.
Scolpitele nel vostro cuore
Stando in casa andando per via.
Coricandovi alzandovi;
Ripetele ai vostri figli.
O vi sfaccia la casa,
La malattia vi impedisca,
I vostri nati torcano il visi da voi.

While the use of a poem or a prayer as an epigraph of a memoir is not unusual, this poem instructs the reader to meditate upon the significance of life in Auschwitz for what it tells us about the capacity of human beings to humiliate their own kind. "Consider," the second stanza of the poem suggests, whether the humiliation endured by the *Häftlinge* (inmates) of the camps made them less than "men" or "women." This suggestion to "consider" is not itself glossed in the poem, but the reader is told, in the first two lines of the next stanza: "Meditate (*meditate*) on these things:/I charge you (*commando*) with these words."[11] Then follows the curse upon those who might fail to "inscribe them in [their] hearts/" while waking and sleeping, at home or abroad, or fail to "repeat them to [their] children."

Or may your house crumble,
Disease afflict you,[12]
Your children turn their faces from you.

It has to be said that this is not the kind of epigraph that one would normally expect to find at the beginning of a "historical" account of a life or a memoir of an episode in a life. The threat of a curse is a kind of speech act quite different from the kind conventionally used as an epigraph; it indicates that the discourse to follow will be anything but a coolly objective account of the facts or a contribution to the documentary record.

Nonetheless, as I have tried to demonstrate in my reading of *Se questo è un uomo* in the journal *Parallax*, the specific *literariness* of Levi's text, that is, its poetic rather than documentary nature, excuses it from the kinds of questions we might ask of it in a court of law.[13] This is not to suggest that it is "fictional," and it certainly does not mean that it is "aesthetic." It is simply to say that it uses literary devices (for example, traditional literary or mythological plot structures—Dante's descent into Hell is the model), figures, and principles of linguistic connection and psychological association more tropological than logical in kind.

Levi uses tropes (such as catachresis, metonymy, irony, synecdoche, etc.) and figures (especially for transforming persons into the kind of "characters" or "types" that one finds in myths, legends, and novels) to depict a real situation in which choice and decision involved the life and death of self and others on a daily basis. In many respects, Levi's text conforms to the principles of the genre of confession, since it is his own exculpation for having survived that he seeks as well as that of others.

But of course it is not only his own redemption that is at issue. Levi's is or purports to be an account of what life and death was like in the concentration camp Auschwitz. It is not an imaginary world, and yet it can scarcely be described except poetically. I have often pointed out that Levi adds nothing in the way of factual information that could not be had in any reference book. Instead of telling us "what happened," he tells us "what it felt like" and what it took in self-humiliation to "survive in Auschwitz."

Are we in the domain of fiction then?

Hardly.

In the preface to the Italian edition of *Se questo è un uomo*, Levi addresses the problem of the genre to which his book belongs: "I recognize," he writes, "and beg forgiveness for the structural defects of the book." But, he adds, "If not actually, in both intention and conception it was born already in the last days of the Lager." The need, he says, "di raccontare agli 'altri,' di fare gli 'altri' partecipi," had assumed among the survivors the "character of a spontaneous (immediate) and violent impulse . . . tanto da rivaleggiare con gli altri bisogni elementari: il libro è stato scritto per soddisfare a questo bisogno; in primo luogo quindi a scopo di liberazione interior."[14] "Whence," he adds, "its fragmentary character; the chapters were written, not in the order of logical succession, but in the order of urgency." The secondary revision, the putting in order and fusion, came later. Thus, Levi with a kind of *captatio benevolentiae* sends his book forth warts and all, as we say. But not before adding a sly warning to the historians:

> "Mi pare superfluo aggiungere che nessumo dei fatti e inventato."[15]

Thus, the work was conceived as if in a dream and then worked out or worked up on reflection and consideration. What does this mean for the factual content of the work? Levi's answer is laconic and ambiguous:

> "It seems superfluous to add that none of the facts was invented."

I cannot resist pointing out that this last sentence can be read in two ways: either "none of the *facts* was invented" (which leaves it open for other things than the facts to have been invented) or "none of the facts was *invented*" (which simply says what we all expect—namely, that the facts were found or given, rather than "made up"). In any event, by this sentence, Levi alerts us to the idea that his discourse is somewhat more or other than either fact or fiction. And why not? By his own account of life in the Lager, the very distinction between fact and fiction had become as nebulous as the distinction between good and evil. Everything existed in that "gray zone" which Levi would limn in his late work *The Drowned and the Saved*. His point was or seems to me to have been that in the world of the Lager, things were as difficult to make sense of as any life in "history."

To sum up: did the experience of the victims, survivors, or casualties of the Holocaust constitute a new kind of experience hitherto unknown to "history"? And if so, what could possibly be said about this experience that would not violate or otherwise diminish the sense of its exceptionality? My suggestion has been that we cannot establish on the basis of any strictly factual account whether the Holocaust was a new event, a new kind of event, or simply an old kind of event with a different face. If it is a new kind of event, an event peculiar to our modernity, then this would account for our unease in the face of conventional historiographical treatments of this event. I have suggested that the straightforward declarative mode favored by traditional historians cannot do justice to the vast mass of witness literature insofar as the historian must ask of it, "Is it true?" I have suggested further that one might want to consider the possibility that the witnesses of the kind of extreme events in which the last (and our own) century abounds might very well be writing or speaking in a different mode of expression, such as the interrogative, the imperative, and the subjunctive. I go further: I suggest that, when it comes to an *artistic* version of witness testimony, such as Levi's *Se questo è un uomo*, the question of the factual truth of the account is of a lesser importance. It is, rather, a question of mode rather than of mimesis.

CHAPTER 3

The Historical Event

For the process of truth to begin, something must happen. What there already is—the situation of knowledge as such—generates nothing other than repetition. For a truth to affirm its newness, there must be a *supplement*. This supplement is committed to chance. It is unpredictable, incalculable. It is beyond what is. I call it an event. A truth thus appears, in its newness, because a supplement interrupts repetition.
—Alain Badiou, *Infinite Thought*

Recent discussion on the periphery of mainstream historical studies has revealed the extent to which "belonging to history" (rather than being "outside of it") or "having a history" (rather than lacking one) have become values attached to certain modern quests for group identity. From the perspective of groups claiming to have been excluded from history, history itself is seen as a possession of dominant groups who claim the authority to decide who or what is to be admitted to history and thereby determine who or what will be considered to be fully human. Even among those groups which pride themselves on belonging to history (here understood as being civilized) or in having a history (here understood as having a real as against a mythical genealogy), it has long been thought that history is written by the victors and to their advantage and that historical writing, consequently, is an ideological weapon with which to double the oppression of already vanquished groups by depriving them of their historical pasts and consequently of their identities as well.

Although it has long been claimed that "history" is a place in and a condition of being of everything that is "truly" human and that "history" is a universal process or relationship (like entropy or gravity), "history" itself shows that "history" was invented and cultivated as a learned science in the West, is based on specifically Western, aristocratic, racist, gen(d)eric, and classist preconceptions, and is no more "universalist" in its applicability to other cultures than Christianity or capitalism. So to view "history" as a "gift" of unalloyed value and usefulness to those who are seeking to enter it or belong to it may be delusory. It is within the context of this problematic that I wish to address the question of the nature, meaning, and discursive function of the historical event.

Let me stress that by the term "history," I mean "the past," to be sure, but also something other and much more. Every individual and every group has a past, just by virtue of having a genetic and a cultural endowment of some kind. But a past made up of a genetic and cultural endowment is not the same thing as a historical past. In our time, which is that of late modernity, a specifically historical past is created by professional or in some way socially authorized investigators of what is only a virtual past as long as it has not been established as having really happened on the basis of evidence of a specific kind and authority. This historical past is a construction made by selecting from the wide range of all the events of the human past a specific congeries of those events that can be established as having happened at specific times and places and can be fitted into diachronically organized accounts of a group's self-constitution over time.

As Michael Oakeshott has argued,[1] this historical past is quite different from "the practical past" which most of us carry around in our heads in the form of memory, imagination, snippets of information, formulas and practices that we perform by rote, and vague ideas about "history" which we draw on in the course of day for the performance of tasks as various as running for president of the United States, justifying a policy of war or economic adventure, planning a party, or arguing a case at law. The historical past exists only in the books and articles written by professional investigators of pasts and written for the most part for one another rather than for the general public. This historical past, according to the doxa of the professionals, is constructed as an end in itself, has very limited if any practical usefulness, and contributes only minimally to the understanding of what ordinary folk regard as "the present." It is ironic that, as professional historical studies have become more and more scientific, they have become less and less useful for any practical purpose, including the traditional one of educating the laity in the realities of political life. Modern historical studies are genuinely dianoetic in aim and method, contemplative rather than active in kind.

For modern historical studies, a historical event is any occurrence that lends itself to investigation by the techniques and procedures currently in force among the guild of professional historians. Such an event may make its appearance in the practical life of a given society or other kind of group, but insofar as it can be studied as a "historical" event, it is moved out of the category of past events that can be utilized for practical purposes and removed into that "historical past" which renders it now only an object of contemplation rather than a tool or instrument to be used in the present for practical ends.

Since the time of Herodotus, there have been conventions, rules, and procedures for deciding what kind of events can be legitimately considered to be "historical," on what grounds and by what kind of evidence events can be established as facts, and how to relate any given historical account of any given body of historical facts to other accounts and facts of a properly historical kind. In modernity, historical events are thought to belong to the class of "natural" events but to be antithetical in kind to "supernatural" events. So, too, historical accounts are thought to belong to the class of narratable[2] processes but to be antithetical to the kind of narratives called "myths" and to any kind of "fiction."

According to the Western *ideology* of history,[3] "history" came into existence at a particular time and place, developed among the peoples inhabiting that time and place, expanded in time and space with the expansion of Western civilization, and in fact is properly recounted as the story of how this expansion into the rest of the world occurred. "Modern" (itself a Western notion and mode of social existence) practitioners of history purport, of course, to have drained the notion of "the historical" of its cultural specificity as a distinctively Western ideology and to have constituted it as a "soft" but nonetheless universal science. But whereas a modern physical science might be taken up by a given culture without necessarily requiring abandonment of dominant traditional values and institutions, it is questionable whether non-Western cultures can take up "history" without jettisoning much of their traditional cultural baggage—any more than non-Western traditional cultures can take up Christianity or capitalism without losing their distinct identities based on their presumed relationship to a past which may have nothing "historical" about it at all.

Thus, "history," or so it might seem, is or has been for most of the last two millenia a *construction* and a value in the West while other cultures have chosen to relate to their pasts in ways sometimes similar to but ultimately different from the "historical" way.[4] It is for this, and a number of other reasons, to be sure, that *theories* of history have been developed in recent times, in the West and elsewhere, directed at the identification of ambiguities of the kind usually ascribed to ideologies, myths, and religions rather than those found in scientific disciplines. In other words, there has been an effort in recent times to "deconstruct" history in much the same way that "man," "race," "gender," "literature," "society," and other mainstays of Western humanism have been deconstructed. Excluded and subaltern groups have objected, of course, to this theorization of history as yet another tactic designed to foreclose their claim to "belong to history" quite as much as their oppressors or to "have a history" of their own that founds their identity similarly.

Yet, theory of history (as against historiological theories or theoretical considerations about the nature and uses of historical knowledge) developed within Western culture at a particular moment in the evolution of historical studies, the moment at which it was professionalized, academicized, and began to lay claim to the status of a (modern) science. There can be no science in the modern sense without theory, and indeed it is a sign of the modernity of a given field of scientific activity to be divisible into a "theoretical" and a "practical" (or "applied") dimension. Prior to this moment in its development, historiographical composition was treated as a perfectly "natural" or ordinary activity that could be practiced by anyone endowed with "letters" and the learning required to read old documents or interrogate witnesses of past events effectively. Prior to this moment, differences might be entertained as to the "meaning" that could be derived from study of past public affairs, especially when claims of a religious or politically sectarian nature regarding certain events of the past were concerned, but these were not so much "theoretical" as, rather, "practical" matters—insofar, especially, as they required the effort to establish "the facts" at issue as a necessary preliminary to the assessment of their possible meaning. To those for whom the Incarnation or the Resurrection or the Descent of the Holy Spirit were already taken *as fact* on faith, the problem of the relation of fact to meaning was already resolved relatively easily.

By contrast, for the scientific historian the only possible factuality to be accorded to these allegedly "miraculous" events would be their status as beliefs held by specific people at specific times and places. The factuality of the events themselves would have to be treated as having been based on evidence of a kind not to be admitted in historical (or, more precisely, historiological) discourse.[5]

Obviously, in cases like the last mentioned, scientific historians would be concerned as much about the nature of the events under question as they would be about the nature of the evidence offered in support of their factuality. In history, any reported event of whatever kind, natural or miraculous as the case might be, has to be treated as a potential fact since to rule out any given reported event as impossible in advance of investigation of the evidence of its occurrence would violate the empiricist principles governing historical inquiry from the origins of the genre. But the very distinction between natural events and miraculous events indicates the importance of the distinction between event and fact in historiological discourse. Since a miraculous event is a manifestation of a power outside of nature and a fortiori outside of history, a miraculous event is the one kind of event that can never be treated as a historical fact.

The canonical version of the distinction between an event and a fact has it that "a fact is an event under a description"—where "description" can be understood as consisting of a perspicuous listing of attributes of the event—or a "predication," by which an event is assigned to its proper kind and, usually, given a proper name.[6] An event cannot enter into a history until it has been established as fact. From which it can be concluded: events happen, facts are established. A fact may be construed as a happening in speech or writing, and in this sense conceived as an event. But facts are events of a special kind: they are events in speech that are about other speech events and other kinds of events beyond or outside of speech. On this account, a historical fact would differ from other kinds of fact by virtue of the rules prevailing in historical discourses for determining when a given event could be described as the kind of event properly characterized as "historical."

Now, in general, people who know something about the issue have little difficulty defining "historical event" and distinguishing historical from other kinds of events: pseudo-events; non-events; natural, supernatural, imaginary, and illusory events, and so on. And historians in general have good or at least tried and trusted rules for determining how events are to be established as facts or established as having really happened rather than only appearing to have happened or as having been falsely reported as having happened. None of these procedures is scientific in the sense of requiring experimental replication of the event under laboratory conditions or the subsumption of a given event to the causal laws or relationships governing the class of events to which it may belong. But they are good enough for the kind of crude social uses to which historical knowledge has been contrived to contribute since its invention in Greece during the fifth century B.C.E.

So, let us grant that there are events and there are facts. Let us grant, too, that there are series of events and structures of events that can be factualized, which is to say, dated, placed, described, classified, and named well enough to permit a distinction between "atomic" or individual facts and something like "molar" or macro-facts—"large" facts such as "The Russian Revolution of 1917" or "big" facts such as "The Renaissance." This would allow us to imagine a wide range of "historical facts" which would make up that "history" which is the object of study of "historians."

But this way of thinking about history—as an aggregation of facts—begs the question of the status of those "events" which are the content, referent, or necessary condition of facts.

There has been a great deal of discussion of late about the event in general and about the historical event specifically. In historiography, the evental status of the Holocaust is a matter of extensive debate: is or was the Holocaust an event unique to history and therefore incomparable to (or incommensurable with) other events of a similar kind? So, too, for the event now called "9/11." Was the attack on the Twin Towers on September 11, 2001, an utterly new kind of event, indeed emblematic of a *new* epoch and paradigmatic therefore of a category of historical events hitherto unimaginable and requiring, consequently, a search for new principles of explanation for its contextualization? Or was it simply an event that happened to have been unexpected in the United States, an event unimaginable in that context—since, obviously, it was all too imaginable among its perpetrators?

In most of these discussions, *that* an event occurred does not have to be established. What is at question is the nature of the event, its relative novelty, the scope and intensity of its impact, and its meaning or what it reveals about the society in which it took place. "Things will never be the same," it has been said of both of the two events; "It is the end of American innocence," it is said of 9/11; "Never again," has been one response to the Holocaust.

While responses such as these are both understandable and, if understood figuratively, more than adequately justified, it is not always registered how such responses implicitly presume a precise idea of what a historical event—as against a natural event—consists of. A natural event, such as an earthquake or an avalanche, will always have been conceivable, imaginable, possible, and, in some locales, even probable. The disastrous consequences of such events attach to the human beings who insufficiently prepared for the occurrence of this type of event in the physical areas affected by them. Thus, although *the effects* of such events on human beings and groups in a particular place can appropriately be described as "disastrous," even "tragic," the same epithets could be used to describe the events themselves in only a figurative way. There are no "disasters" and certainly no "tragedies" in nature. The fact that there are plenty of events in history to which such epithets can be legitimately or at least appropriately applied tells us something about the extent to which "history," in spite of its efforts to become scientific, remains indentured to mythical notions of the cosmos, the kinds of events that occur in it, and the kinds of knowledge we can have of them.

In our time, many other events made possible by new technologies and modes of production and reproduction have changed the nature of institutions and practices that had remained virtually unchanged for millenia (for example, warfare and health care) and changed them so radically that it has become impossible to write a history of, say, war as a tale of *continuous* development from the Stone Age to only yesterday. Weapons of mass destruction cause a quantum leap in the *history* of warfare. Antibiotics and genetic engineering change definitively the nature of health care for the foreseeable future. All this suggests that the principles that make historical change possible in the first place may themselves undergo change. Or to put it another way: change itself changes, at least in history if not in nature. If it does, then so too can the nature of events change as well.[7]

Can we imagine a new *kind* of event breaking in on our world which might manifest evidence of another, alternative system of existence that differs utterly from our own? Fantasies of alien cultures in outer space and theories of parallel or antithetical universes reflect the wish, hope, or fear of the existence of such alternative places from which new and strange events might emanate. Such fantasies may seem delusory, but they are no more so than our notion of "history" considered as a process made up of conflicting and mutually exclusive societies, cultures, and races each vying with the other for lebensraum and the resources to allow one or another to prevail over all contenders.

But not only that: history itself, with its division into past and present, parses human nature into earlier and later avatars whose differences are often thought to be more striking than any similarities between them, already contains more than enough evidence of radical discontinuity over time. Indeed, history is thought to be composed of events of a kind that effect changes in the common human substrate that amount more to mutations than simply variations on the common heritage. Imagine how different is the kind of event which modernist technology is capable of producing from those that might have been familiar to a peasant of the twelfth century. Certain events in modernity—space travel, genetic engineering, atomic weaponry—are so utterly different from anything previously thought possible that even a *modern* peasant or bourgeois might be forgiven for taking them as "miracles."

So different, indeed, are certain events of the present moment from anything preceding them that we can readily understand why certain intellectuals might be impelled to speak of "the end of history" or, like Marx, speak of everything that has happened up until now as "prehistory" or a prelude to the real drama of a humankind that has finally come into its own and escaped what we had thought of as history *and* nature before.

To be sure, Western historical studies have just recently recovered from a sustained attack, mounted from within its own ranks, on the very notion of "event." I will not recapitulate details of the attack by the Annales School in the decades following World War II upon the fetishistic nature of the historical event and the mythical nature of the idea that historical processes possess the kind of coherence found in stories, fables, and legends. Modern(ist) philosophers of history typically distinguish between a tradition of conventional, popular, or amateur historiography centered on events and concerned to dramatize them, on the one side, and a more scientific and enlightened historiography centered on structures, long-term processes ("la longue durée"), and "slow" time, on the other. "Event-history," it was held, was little more than entertainment and little less than fantasy insofar as it fed the dreams and illusions of a bankrupt humanism. In fact, the French historian Fernand Braudel spent a fair amount of time trying to diminish the focus on the event in historical research because he saw it as the mainstay of a narrativist approach to history, which made it into an element of a drama and substituted emotional gratification for the intellectual satisfaction of science in the process.[8]

As a matter of fact, however, the historiological notion of event is much closer to the dramatic or rather the dramatistic than it is to any possible scientific conception thereof. Historical narratives run much too smoothly to support any claim to realistic representation of the events they feature as their subject-matter. Unlike the kind of natural events (or sets of events) studied by the physical sciences, real historical events run rather roughly and raggedly, largely as a result of the intervention of human agents and agencies into the courses they were originally meant to follow.

Here we encounter another topos in the modernist discourse on the event, that which distinguishes between natural events and historical events on the basis of the presence of human beings, their motivations, their intentions, their desires, their drives, in their enactment. Drama, like epic, is a *mode* of oral, imagistic, gestural, or literary presentation which sets forth an action as a *series* of events within a finite scene, but differs from epic in the assignment of different degrees of significance to events in such a way as to permit the series to be grasped as a *sequence* with a beginning, middle, and end. A historical sequence is periodized or parsed into acts and scenes, each of which is related to what follows as a realization or fulfillment of what had come before. But this raises the question: what is the difference between an event which terminates and one which begins a sequence? Or: is a historical event a sign of a rupture in a series and a point of *metamorphosis* from one level, phase, or aspect of the historical continuum to another? Or is it a sign of *transition* from one phase of a continuum to another?

So much is suggested by Alain Badiou's metaphysical discussion of event in *Being and Event*, a discussion neatly summarized in *Infinite Thought*.[9] He assumes that being is everything that is the case and that there is nothing that is not the case. Nothing new can ever be added to being and therefore no event—understood as an eruption of something coming from outside the totality of being—could ever take place. And yet events *seem* to take place all the time, at least to observers or chroniclers of happenings in the real world. This "seeming to take place" could be construed as an event, but it would belong to consciousness rather than to the world exterior to it.

So how is this kind of event possible? As I understand it, Badiou thinks that events *seem* to occur because there is a disparity between being, on the one side, and the knowledge of being, on the other. Event occurs when knowledge of some hitherto unknown aspect of being has to be added to what had been previously known about being. It is, as it were, this "shock" to the knowledge-system by the insistent nature of a newly discovered truth about being that registers as an event to consciousness. In reality, Badiou argues, a new bit of knowledge is only apparently new: it is like the discovery of a hitherto-unknown prime number in mathematics. It was always "there" (which is to say, was always "nowhere" but among the universe of numbers) only awaiting (as it were) for that computer which is endlessly generating new prime numbers of all but infinite length for its registration. As thus envisaged, event is like the sudden awareness that what had been thought of as the last prime number was only the next to the last and, in fact, is, as the computer continues to spit out new prime numbers, rapidly shrinking in rank and substance with each new prime—the penultimate prime number moves down or back as the newest prime appears.

Now, all this would seem to have little to do with any possible understanding of events that occur in ordinary daily experience (whatever that is) or as envisaged by conventional wisdom or by such "practical" disciplines as those cultivated in the human and social sciences. And this is because it is already generally presumed that event merely indicates an occurrence *unanticipated* by current knowledge about the world and its processes.

For example, the important question about events occurring in what Paul Veyne calls "the sublunary world" of "history" is whether any given event is assimilable to one or another of the received knowledge systems available to a given community or whether the event in question requires the revision or even the total abandonment of the system previously thought capable of adequately identifying, classifying, and determining any event's "propriety."[10] If there is any metaphysical dimension to this notion of event, it attaches to the status of "history" understood as a sphere of existence inhabited by human beings and subject to laws or principles that belong to but deviate slightly from those that govern the rest of "nature." To be sure, knowledge of this "history" does not include all of the human beings that have ever lived or will have lived over the course of worldly time. Knowledge of history is always fragmentary, incomplete, and partial, which is one reason that events of a specifically "historical" kind can occur and will continue to occur and indeed cannot not occur for the "foreseeable" future. But the historical event begins to look suspiciously like the kind of event which Badiou characterized as a "supplement" to being-in-general. It depends on the positing of a knowledge of being and therefore a knower of it as a condition of possibility of its occurrence. Which means that specifically historical events could not occur before a specifically historical kind of knowledge existed. It would have no ground or context against which to display its newness.

On the other hand, a historical event will appear as new only insofar as it can be recognized as inherently or substantively or potentially belonging to the class of events already recognized as "historical" but is apprehended, at the same time, as being exotic to that class. As thus envisaged, any "new" historical event seems to be both in and out of "the historical." Here is where "historical research" enters: its aim is to establish whether the new event belongs to "history" or not, or whether it is some other kind of event. The event in question need not be new in the sense of having only recently arrived to historical consciousness—the event may have already been registered as having happened in legend, folklore, or myth, and it is, therefore, a matter of identifying its historicity, narrativizing it, and showing its propriety to the structure or configuration of the context in which it appeared. An example and even a paradigm of this situation would be the well-known "search for the historical Jesus" or the establishment of the historicity (or ahistoricity) of the "Jesus" who was represented in the Gospels, not only as a worker of miracles but as Himself the supreme miracle of miracles, the Messiah or God Incarnate whose death and resurrection can redeem the world.

The idea that historical events could not have occurred before the idea of history and the category of the historical had been invented is only a logical paradox. Any right-thinking person would know that the idea of history and the category of the historical must have arisen from somebody's reflection on the kind of events which manifestly differed from some other kind of event, so that the term "history" and the category of "the historical" must derive their meaning from their references to this special kind of event. But let us try to imagine a time before which the idea of history and the category of the historical existed, a time when a number of different kinds of events had been identified but not events of the historical kind. On the evidence available, it seems that the Greeks, who are supposed to have invented the idea of history as an inquiry into the past and the genre of history writing as an account of past events established by such inquiry as having happened, apparently had no word with the signified of our word for "history."

Thus, the Greek "istoría" will start by meaning only "inquiry" and then, by metonymy of result for the activity that produces it, come to mean the "findings" resulting from the inquiry and, beyond that, by synecdoche, become a name—"the history"—for the events described in the account understood as "what happened in the (or a) past"—or something like that. The Greek word for happenings in the past was "ta gegenemena" but the term most used to name an *account* of past happenings (whether based on "inquiry" or received tradition) was "logos." Whence Thucydides's dismissal of Herodotus as a (mere) "logographer" or teller of stories about the past in order to distinguish what he himself was doing in his "inquiries" into the past and analyses of its processes.

And it should be noted that "logographer" was the term used to characterize an inquirer into the *recent* past in contrast to what might be called (according to Antonin Liakos) an "archaio-lographer" who investigated the remote or *remote* past.[11] Thucydides investigated the recent rather than the remote past in order to identify the causes of the wars between Athens and Sparta, so he would qualify as a logographer as much as Herodotus. But his inquiry was not more systematic than that of Herodotus, only differently so—inasmuch as he seems to have used principles of Hippocratean medicine to serve as a model for how to read the symptoms of the plague that destroyed or fatally weakened the Greek city-states and their empires, while Herodotus was content with the kind of general principles enunciated in pre-Socratic philosophy for his explanations of the events he recounted (explanations of the "what goes up must come down" variety). It was the *kind* of systematicity he used that earned for Thucydides the (modern) title of the first "scientific" historian. Which might be taken to mean that he not only placed events in stories but also provided an argument for their relevance to his aim of explaining the causes and effects of the events he was investigating.

On this account, Herodotus can be credited with having invented the specifically historical event and suggesting its difference from the kinds of events that derived from the actions of gods and spirits. Thucydides can then be credited with having invented a version of historical method or procedures for studying and analyzing, rather than merely reporting, what happened in the past in order to understand the present. But whether he was actually "doing" history or bringing a new method to the analysis of the kinds of events Herodotus had investigated, is a moot point, it being undecidable whether specifically "historical" events are subsumable under general laws or not. In any case, it was left to the Romans to provide the word "historia"—with its primary meaning of tale or story understood as the *kind* of account "proper" to the rendition of a series of events into a "history"— with a basis for the notion of the historical event as the kind of event which, although occurring in real rather than imaginary life, could legitimately be presented in the form(s) of the *kinds* of tales and fables previously told of gods, demons, ghosts, heroes, and other such supernatural beings. With this development, I would suggest, the idea of history as a *truthful* account of events that *really* happened in the past cast in the form of *story* with a *plot* is achieved. And this provides at least one way of identifying a specifically historical event. As Paul Ricoeur puts it: a historical event is a real event capable of serving as an element of a "plot." Or, as Louis O. Mink used to say: a historical event is one that can truthfully be described in such a way as to serve as an element of a narrative.[12]

All this implies that events are not made "historical" solely by virtue of having really happened, having happened in a specific time in the past and at a specific place in this world, and having had some identifiable effect on the contexts into which they erupted. And this is because a list of such events, even a list of events in chronological order, might constitute an annals or a chronicle but hardly a history. In order for a given singular event, set, or series of events to qualify as "historical," the event, set, or series must also be validly describable as if they had the attributes of elements in a *plot* of a story.[13]

Now, the mention of the word "plot" raises another specter which, for professional historians, is almost as threatening as the word "myth." Not only because the word "plot" is the English translation of the Greek "mythos," but also because "plot" is typically thought to be the device which gives to literary fictions their explanatory effect.[14] The debate over how the insertion of an event into a series in such a way as to transform it into a sequence and provide thereby some equivalent of an explanation for its occurrence is a long one and too long even to summarize here. Suffice to say that, for our purposes, plot or what I have chosen to call emplotment is common to all the kinds of narrative discourse: mythical, fictional, or historical. Thus, it is possible to say that, if myths, fictional stories, and histories share a common form (the story, fable, tale, parable, allegory, whatever), they also share a common content, which, following Frank Ankersmit, we may call "narrative substance."[15] The concept of "narrative substance" allows us to say that the historical event, unlike the natural event," is narratable.[16]

The *doxa* of modern professional historical research has it that there are no plots *in* history (the events of the past) any more than there could be a large, all-encompassing, overall plot *of* History (in the sense of a plan, or predetermined end, aim, purpose, or telos of the whole trajectory of human development, from the obscure origins to the unimaginable end). The objection to the so-called "master narratives" of history, the rejection of which, according to Lyotard, is supposed to be the dominant characteristic of postmodernist thought, was that such fantastic notions as "providence," "fate," "destiny," "progress," "the dialectic," and so on were nothing but residues of mythical and religious dreams of the kind long left behind by "modernity." The general objection to the "master narratives" was that they represented a kind of *teleological* thinking that had had to be overcome for the modern sciences of nature to take shape. There is no teleology in nature and inasmuch as history belongs to nature (rather than the reverse)—or so it was thought—there could be no teleology in history. And this included local as well as universal history.

To be sure, human beings and human groups typically *think* teleologically, which is to say, make plans for current and future activities in the light of envisioned ends, aims, purposes. One could speak of human intentions as end-oriented and, indeed, in a way that permitted one to use *intentionality* as a basis for distinguishing human from animal nature. But, as the poet says, "the best laid plans of mice and men . . . ," and the *doxa* tells us, "the road to perdition is paved with good intentions." Human beings and institutions may very well plan their activities and practices with an end in view, but to suggest that the destinies of individuals and groups can be predetermined in the way the destiny of an oak tree is predetermined by the acorn from which it springs is a possibility at once comforting and horrifying. Comforting because it takes responsibility away from the subject-agent of history, horrifying because it takes responsibility away from the subject-patient of history. Besides, as it is said, determinism is always what governs other people, never one's own self—except when one wishes to avoid responsibility for a specific action.

But what if it is possible that human beings are both free and determined, responsible and not responsible, at one and the same time for their actions? To think in this way is, of course, a scandal for the philosopher and foolishness for the man of common sense. And yet . . .

Near the origin of Western philosophy and specifically in the legendary teachings of the founder of Stoicism, Zeno of Citium (d. 265 B.C.E.), we encounter the association of the notion of "event" with that of "destiny" which was to become a commonplace of thought about time on down to Heidegger, Ricoeur, and Badiou. Zeno seems to have taught that every incident occurring in the life of a person was interpretable as evidence of providence's working to turn what would otherwise be a meaningless jumble of events into a destiny (with its sense that the end of a life occurs not only at a particular time but also at a particular place—whence our notion of a *destin*ation as the place we are headed toward).

Here, to be sure, the terms "event" and "destiny" are translated into the elements of a drama with a presumed beginning, middle, and end, a denouement, and a falling off of action after the scene of recognition (*anagnorisis*); and they function more as schemata than as concepts, elements of consciousness that encompass both myth and science, and exude the odor of narrative as well as that of argument. Of course, etymology *explains* nothing, but the mythological relation between event and destiny indicates the ways in which, in poetic thinking, a problematical term like "event," with its connotation of both meaningfulness and meaninglessness, can function as an operator in a process in which an *image* of formal coherency (destiny, fate, *moira*, *telos*) can be used to endow chaos with cosmos. In any event, the relating of event to destiny as figure to fulfillment gave me some insight into what was, to me, a lexicographical surprise: my *Roget*'s treatment of "destiny" as an *antonym* of "event."[17]

I was looking for the antonym of "event," because I wanted to begin my thought about the historical event by placing it within the matrix of Aristotle's hermeneutic square, in order to discern what might be its contradictories, contraries, and implicants.[18] If "event" is treated as a concept, then, precisely because it is a concept, it must have an opposed or antithetical term which tells us what would be its contradictory. The convention which sets "event" in a relationship of contradictoriness to "destiny" suggests that, perhaps, an event can at least be known to be related to the field of, on, or against which it happens, as a "part" of a process *can be opposed* to the "whole" of which it is a part. The event can never be the whole of the process of which it is a part, because "destiny" names the whole process of which any given event is only a part.

But then that leaves us with the problem of identifying the *contrary* of event's antithetical term, "destiny," which must be, according to Aristotle's way of reasoning, the "non-destinal," or anything that is not headed anywhere, has no proper place, no substance, and is therefore only a pseudo-event, an element of a pseudo-destiny.[19] And this suggests that whatever an event will finally turn out to be, the one thing that we can say about it is that it is not destiny, that it is not the whole process which might ultimately endow contingency with meaning, the meaning of *place* in a sequence, placefulness, or situ-ation. This is to say that the event is not and can never be the whole of whatever it is a part, element, or factor—except at the end, when it comes into its own or finds a place it was destined to come to at last. Maybe this is what Heidegger had in mind when he spoke of history as *Dasein*'s "on-the-way-ness" to a place it would never reach and *Dasein*'s fate as "eine Verwindung," a meandering, a wending, a drift, slide, or roaming that always ends short of a destination, because destiny implies propriety and mankind is "ohne Eigenschaften."[20]

But now, in order to fill out our form of reasoning, we must posit the *contrary* (not the contradictory) of event itself and if, as we have already indicated, it cannot be either the whole (which is destiny) or those other parts of the whole besides itself, then the event must be something else, which is neither part nor whole of the whole, which can only be, I think, some combination of the non-evental and non-destinal. Whence, I presume, the modern(ist) juxtaposition of event and structure as a model for a scientific construal of the nature of the historical. In modernist thinking, structure stands in for destiny, providence, fate, fortune, and the like, insofar as—as in the structuralist paradigm—the "meaning" of things human must turn out to be nothing other than their form, raised up against a "nature" which, more and more, reveals its meaning as little more than "chaos." In this model, the event is what disturbs structure, whatever it is that resists incorporation into what is at any given moment "the case." From an ontological point of view, every event is an embarrassment and a challenge, an embarrassment to the comprehensiveness of structure and a challenge to structure's power to provide meaning to everything that is the case. Small wonder that structuralism has turned out to be the very antithesis of a historical world-view. As a plenum of events each one of which is an individual happening (a kind of "concrete universal" resistant to subsumption to any universal, on the one hand, and to reduction to an aggregate of particularities, on the other), history appears to be little more than the condition from which any structuralist would wish to escape.

Now, all of this could be quite bewildering if it were not for the fact that, outside the various fields of historical studies and in those disciplines where something like a "historical method" remains a principal component in their operations, the notion of the event has been pretty much discredited as an element of scientific thought. The notion of event remains a staple of a certain kind of literary writing, of the novel, of the romance, of poetry, of theology, and of myth, and so on—kinds of composition called "imaginative" or "imaginary" and generally related by genealogical affiliation to pre-scientific ways of thinking, explaining, and living with the world rather than living off of it. And indeed there is a whole body of contemporary writing which suggests that the notion of event and especially the notion of event informing and authorizing a belief in the reality of "history" is a displacement from mythical modes of thinking and actually has more in common with a religious idea of miracle than with any scientific conception of what an event could possibly be.

This body of contemporary writing has its origins in the hybrid genre of the "historical novel" which, contrary to the rules of the game just being formulated by the historical profession, faces openly the problem of the relation between the past and the present, the ambiguity of "the recent past," and the paradox of the presence of the past in the present—as in Scott, Manzoni, and Dumas, but also Balzac, Stendhal, Flaubert, Dickens, Tolstoy, Thackeray, Trollope, Conrad, and a host of lesser lights. It is the historical novel which lays the groundwork of the modernist novel in which the event begins to dissipate and the line between the past and the present becomes as scumbled as that between consciousness and the unconscious. Modernism, for all its trumpeting of the novelty of "the way we live now," restores the dignity of the archaic, formerly abandoned by history because of its lack of documentation and consigned to the tender mercies of archaeology and the "antiquities," as a source of meaning for "reality."

As Auerbach and others argue, modernism is anything but a flight from realism and history. It liberates the historical event from the domesticating suasions of "plot" by doing away with "plot" itself. Moreover, far from abandoning reality for fantasy, modernism shows how much of the fantastic is contained in "the real." Modernism not only extends the reach of the historical event horizontally, allowing it to wash into adjacent areas of time, it reveals the depths of the historical event, showing how many layers of meaning it conceals, how labile are its pulsions, how resistant to concretion it is.

Modernism probes the depths of the historical event in much the same way that psychoanalysis probes the depths of the psychic event,[21] and indeed changes the relation between the event and its context by dissolving the line between them. All of which adds up to the creation of a new mode of literary writing in which the line between factual discourse and fictional discourse is blurred in a kind of writing (the infamous "écriture") that would destroy the artistic authority of the earlier, nineteenth-century realism. Henceforth, history, the historical event, and historicality itself are taken over by a new kind of writing which, for want of a better term, we may call postmodernist.[22]

However, it is not enough to summon up a "new kind of writing" to account for changes in the way that "history" and its typical content "event" are construed in our time. For a distinctively "historical" way of accounting for the invention of a "new kind of writing" requires us to identify the new "content" or phenomenon for the representation of which the new kind of writing is thought to be adequate. I have already alluded to "the modernist event" as such a content, phenomenon, or referent. Now I will go further and suggest that the "substance" of the "content" of this new kind of event is provided in the historiotheticized idea of "trauma."

I cannot end this account of the historical event without a reference to what is often taken to be a new kind of historical event, what is called "the traumatic event." The modern provenance of the term "traumatic" is medicine, where it is used to characterize a wound, more precisely a penetration of the skin and bone, and the resultant scar, physical and psychical, caused by the penetration. When used to characterize a certain kind of historical event, the term "trauma" and its adjectival form "traumatic" are quite conventional and mean something like a massive blow to a social or political system that requires the kind of adjustment, adaptation, or reaction that any organism must make if it is to survive it.

In the theory of psychoanalysis, however, the terms "trauma" and "traumatic" are used (metaphorically, at first) to indicate a shock to the organism that has the somatic and/or psychical effect of "unbinding" the "drives" formerly held in some kind of equilibrium and producing thereby neurotic or psychopathic states (such as paranoia, hysteria, obsessiveness) resulting in the disfunctionality of the organism. This physicalist conception of trauma (developed by Breuer and Freud in the 1890s) does not differ in any special way from its historiological counterpart in which the historical event is viewed as a significant disturbance of a historical (social) system which throws its institutions, practices, and beliefs into disarray and results in group behaviors similar to those manifested in the conditions of hysteria, paranoia, fetishism, and the like.

But Freud and other psychoanalysts later developed another idea of trauma which presupposed a distinctly "historical" element inasmuch as it involved an element of "afterwardness" (*Nachträglichkeit*) understood as a "(temporally) deferred effect" on the organism strikingly similar to what historiology took to be a specifically *historical* relation between the past and the present. For now, Freud characterized the psychic dimension of trauma as not only a (sudden and disruptive) shock to the organism but one that left *in the psyche of certain kinds of individuals* a kind of place devoid of meaning until, under the press of a later event similar in aspect to the original experience of incursion, this place was suddenly enlivened or animated so as to disclose a meaning so overdetermined as to wound the organism once more—in fact, render it doubly wounded, first, by the recall of the original scene of incursion and the sudden discovery of its meaning, and then, by a repetition once more of the original move of fending it off from consciousness, now attended, as it were, by feelings of guilt for not having recognized what it had been in the first place.

There is a similarity between the way historians conceive the relationship between the historical past and the present, on the one side, and Freud's conception of the relationship between a traumatic event in the life of an individual and its "return" to consciousness at some later time but with an impact strong enough to render the individual dysfunctional. The idea of the traumatizing event permits Freud to postulate a "secret history" of an individual and, by extension, of a whole people or nation, against which the "official" account of its past is to be comprehended as an alibi or sublimation in response to guilt feelings derived from the original act. In *Moses and Monotheism* ("Der Mann Moses und die Monotheistische Religion") the theory of the traumatizing historical event permits Freud to postulate a terrible crime in the Hebrew past: the murder of Moses by the people he had saddled with an impossible obligation to the Law, which accounts for the perfervid asceticism, self-discipline, failure to become a nation, restless wandering, guilt, and melancholy of the Jewish people. It is "the return of the repressed memory" of this primal crime—the murder of the Father—that constitutes the past-in-the-present which the Jews at least live as "history."[23]

To be sure, Freud's notion of the "history" of the Hebrew people bears all the marks of myth—in spite of the gestures it makes to current historical scholarship and his own efforts to sound "scientific." But the idiom of mythagogy is utterly appropriate for the kind of cause-effect relationship between past and present which he calls *nachträglich* (belated). It is "magical" involving as it does such notions as action at a distance, deferred effect, latency, and the like. Freud does not reject or question the conventional historical idea that an event at a given time and place "spreads out," as it were, in both time and space, producing other events to be treated as "effects" of a prior "cause." But he does postulate another kind of event, the true nature and effects of which get buried in individual and collective memory, lie latent therein for an indeterminate amount of time, and then, in response to some later event of similarly invasive effect, resurfaces in a *form* that at once reveals and conceals its remote prototype. Such an event, the traumatic event, has the structure of the figure-fulfillment model of Hebrew *and* Christian theodicy.

In the figure-fulfillment model, a *significant* historical event will be recognized by its double occurrence, the first time as an *intimation* of a possibility of meaning and the second time as an "expletion," a filling out or a fulfillment of what was only implicit or, to use a psychological term, latent in the earlier event. The theological models are well known: the substitution of the ram for Isaac in Abraham's intended sacrifice of his son is an anticipation of the Law of Moses which "fulfills" it; the Fall of Adam which is fulfilled in the Resurrection of Christ, and so on. A secularized equivalent of the figure-fulfillment model in historiological theory would be something like the argument that the remote but determinant cause of the French Revolution was the Protestant Reformation. In Tocqueville's argument, the Reformation already contains in embryo, as it were, the Revolution which brings down the Old Regime. Mind you, it is not that the earlier event predetermines the later event, or that the later event is to be considered the telos toward which everything tends once the Reformation has occurred. This is not a teleological idea of historical causation. No one could have predicted the outbreak of the French Revolution on the basis of whatever knowledge they might have had about the Reformation. It is only after the Revolution had occurred that it became possible to see what the Reformation had made possible.

So it is with Freud's so-called "traumatic" or "traumatizing" event. There is no absolute necessity for an early molestation of a child by an adult to surface in later life as "trauma" and produce debilitating effects in the adolescent or adult. It all depends upon the occurrence of a second event similar to the earlier one but openly identifiable as what it is or intended to be that triggers the recognition-repression response that now buries or otherwise blocks access to both events and relegates them to a space outside of the "real history" to which they belong. The equivalent in real history would be a kind of schizo-historiology in which the desire to know or obsession with the past is attended by an equally strong aversion to or rejection of any knowledge of the past that threatens the benign version of historical reality constructed as a screen against the threatening truth. I do not have time to go into the matter now, but I would suggest that Kantorowicz's theory of "the king's two bodies" analyzes a topos of such schizo-history.

It should be stressed, of course, that Freud was neither a professional historian nor a professional philosopher (of history) and that neither professional historians nor professional philosophers had any particular reason to regard his concept of the traumatic event as a contribution to the scientific study of history, the historical past, or the historical relation between the past and the present. On the contrary, it may well be that Freud borrowed contemporary myths or notions about history as a model for how to conceptualize a relation between the past and the present of a given individual or nation or people or indeed any group whatsoever in order to conceptualize the kind of relation between present and past he wished to call "traumatic." Freud was an amateur or dilettante in history, archaeology, and anthropology and he was interested in any kind of knowledge that could be turned to therapeutic use in the treatment of psychologically induced maladies. In other words, he was interested in "the practical past" rather than in the historical past composed by and distilled into the learned tomes of professional historians, anthropologists, and archaeologists for the enlightenment of their professional peers.[24]

So although he used the work of professional scholars in other fields of inquiry, he was less interested in contributing to those fields of study than in using whatever of their lore that could be helpful in conceptualizing a possible treatment for individuals (and groups) suffering from the malady known at that time as "melancholy," a depressive condition that became chronic when an individual sustained an unthinkable loss of a loved object which the normal or conventional modes of "mourning" failed to alleviate.

Now, the important theoretical point about Freud's psychoanalytical concept of trauma consists in the fact that, according to Freud himself, there is no such thing as an inherently traumatic *event*. Even the most horrendous kind of loss is responded to by different individuals in different ways, some in the mode of traumatization, others in the mode of mourning, still others in the various modes of sublimation, repression, or symbolization that take place in the process of "working through" the experience of loss. And here it is necessary to stress again the differences between a medical or physiological notion of trauma and the psychological, psychosomatic, or psychoanalytical idea of it. From a physicalist point of view there could be inherently traumatic events, which would be any event of sufficiently violent force to threaten the destruction of the organism, individual or collective. That such a notion of historical event already exists in the repertory of professional historians is indicated by their use of the concept of "crisis" as a condition through which groups as well as individuals can suffer. But from the standpoint of the psychoanalytical notion of trauma, there are crises and there are crises. Not all crises, especially the physical ones endured by the organism, are traumatizing of the groups or individuals affected by them. Indeed, trauma names only a particular kind of response to crisis, the way in which it is (only) apperceived rather than perceived as the thievery of self that it will later, under the press of a similar event, be both perceived and understood to have been. What could be a more "historical," "historiological," or "historiographical" way of construing the specifically "historical event"? Or to put it another way: what could be a more historiological way of construing a certain kind of psychosomatic event (whether the soma in question be that of an individual or that of a group)?

It is possible that the specifically historical event is a happening that occurs in some present (or in the experience of a living group), the nature of which cannot be discerned and a name given to it because it manifests itself only as an "eruption" of a force or energy that disrupts the ongoing system and forces a change (the direction or trajectory of which is unknowable until it is launched or entered upon), the end, aim, or purpose of which can only be discerned, grasped, or responded to at a later time. But not just any old "later time." Rather, that later time when the eruption of what seems to be in some way affiliated with an earlier event reveals or seems to reveal in the fact of that affiliation the "meaning," significance, gist, even foretelling, though in a masked and obscure way, both of the original event and the later one. Such that the later event can be plausibly represented in a narrative in which it is the fulfillment (or de-realization) of the meaning having lain latent and now made manifest retrospectively in the earlier one.

If that turned out to be the case, it would be . . . a miracle.

CHAPTER 4

Contextualism and Historical Understanding

In this essay I am going to presuppose—following the lead of the philosopher Arthur Danto—that *understanding* is a kind of "explanation by recognition," a feeling that an object *adequately described* has been shown to occupy a place proper to it in the system of nomination and classification provided by the "common sense" (and/or the historical culture) of a given time and place. For example, a description of a battle that occurred in a remote time, a distant place, and under cultural circumstances different from those prevailing in the time, place, and culture in which the description of it is being composed will be a product of translation procedures that mediate between different styles of imaging, on the one hand, and different languages, codes, or structures for identifying and classifying it, on the other. Needless to say, since we are dealing specifically with *historical* descriptions (descriptions cast in the idiom of historiology) or—and this is not quite the same thing—descriptions *of* historical phenomena (which is to say, phenomena that have already been designated and classified as possessing a substance of "historicality"), I will concentrate on *verbal* descriptions, which is to say, verbal descriptions of entities in the past intended to conjure up a mental image or picture thereof (on the basis of a "historiological" study of written and monumental evidence deemed sufficient to establish the reality and the nature of changes occurring in a given entity in a given time and place in the past). The features and structures of such images can be "recognized" as the kind of features and structures that any literate person of any culture or linguistic endowment would look for in an effort to identify and classify anything appearing alien—or in the present case, simply "past"—to the "space of experience" of their own time.[1]

Since it is *verbal* descriptions we are speaking about, we might wish to call upon the distinctions drawn in modern semiotics among indexical, iconological, and symbolic sign systems in order to characterize the different *kinds* of descriptions met with in discourses such as historiography, ethnography, travel writing, biography, testimony, novels, jurisprudence, and, yes, even philosophy. Historiographical descriptions are normally thought of as being of at least two kinds: first, *technical*, in which the idiom used to represent a given historeme or unit of historiological interest functions as a metalanguage with specific signifieds assigned to specific signifiers such that any entity deemed indescribable in terms of the code specified is automatically ruled out as a possible object of historiological inquiry; and secondly, *natural* or *commonsensical* descriptions, in which the rules of usage and mention of things "historical" are those of everyday educated speech and, it must be added, both utilitarian and artistic writing. (For example, in modern historiography, miracles and ghosts are ruled out as possible objects of historiological inquiry—except when it is a matter of trying to understand why people of an earlier or different time believed such things to be possible.)

Descriptions of things purporting to be "scientific" are typically cast in a technical language, and it is characteristic of historiography seeking to emulate or utilize one or another of the social sciences to be cast in technical language or jargon even when it is primarily descriptive rather than explanatory (or nomological) in intent.[2] But even after historical studies first sought to become "scientific," the mainline of professional historiography remained committed to the protocols and conventions of ordinary, educated speech as its preferred idiom of presentation. This was especially true of narrative historiography, which is to say, historiography that wishes to *represent* veridically congeries of historical events established as having occurred in the same time-space ("chronotopical")[3] locale, as possessing the manifest *form* of the kinds of *stories* met with in myth, epic, legend, and fable but without detracting in any way from the "factuality" of the events thus treated. And for some historians the presentation of events in the form of a "true" story constitutes a kind of explanation of "things as they really happened" or "things as they were" in the past. Thus, in seeking to characterize the cognitive force or value of narrative historiography as a description, we must get beyond the idea that "description" is an interruption of "narrative" and recognize that, *grosso modo*, narrative history is itself a description of a world in which significant processes manifest themselves in the form of stories. And that in narrative histories the story told is intended to be taken as a description which explains by the emplotment of events as *recognizable* as a story of a particular kind: tragic, comedic, romantic, epical, farcical, and so on, as the case may be.

In my opinion, this idea is plausible, because in most if not all cultures a narrativization or narrativized account of how anything has come to be what it has realistically or commonsensically or artistically been taken to be counts as an "explanation" of that thing even if, lacking explicit designation of the causal laws that determine its natural order of being, it still would not count as a *scientific* explanation. But the problem with any attempt to assess a description (or even explanation) of an object presumed to be located "in history" or simply in "the past" is that there is no state of affairs or situation that can be invoked as an "original" body of phenomena against which different descriptions of what they are thought to have been can be compared and assessed as to their relative accuracy, precision, and truthfulness. When it comes to *past* states of affairs, there exist no undescribed congeries of phenomena with which to compare those versions offered in different descriptions of it. As Louis O. Mink has pointed out, when it comes to trying to compare different descriptions of *the same* phenomena in the past, it is difficult to comprehend what "the same" might mean. For, of the past there are no phenomena to observe either in their raw or in any predescriptively processed state.

This problem of the unobservable referent is not mitigated by the contention that the state of affairs postulated as "original" is to be found in the documents and monuments serving as the "sources" of the historiological operation. And this is because, although these sources do exist in the present and in a mode of being that allows them to be perceived, read, studied, and criticized as to *their* relative accuracy, precision, relevance, and truthfulness with respect to the matters of which *they* speak, the sources seldom yield unalloyedly consistent accounts of "what happened" in the chronotopical domains from which they have descended. In other words, the problem with the sources is the same as that with the original state of affairs against which we would wish to measure the relative realism and truthfulness of any given account thereof. One can compare different descriptions of what may be agreed to have been a common referent, but one would have to describe a previously undescribed state of affairs in the past in order to use this as the referent against which the different descriptions under critical consideration could be assessed as to their truth, relevance, or adequacy.

Now, it is here that the idea of "context" can be used effectively to mitigate the tendency to skepticism to which the elusiveness of the historical referent may conduce. Recall that "context" derives, first, from theories of sacred (and later, literary) texts in which the term denotes the "speech, writing, or print that normally precedes and follows a word or other element of language" in a patch of writing and has to do with the difference in meaning that may occur when a word is quoted "out of context" versus its meaning as affected by the words preceding and following it (its context) in a given usage. When extended to refer to nonlinguistic or extratextual elements of the surround of a word, idea, or concept, "context," as *The Oxford Concise Dictionary* has it, often refers to "a situation," such that any "meaning expressed in terms of context" can then be termed "reference," as against "sense," which "exists in and among language elements regardless of context." The OCD goes on to say: "To illustrate the meaning of 'ram' by pointing to a picture or an animal is to use context, but to define it as 'male sheep' in contrast with 'ewe' is to do so by means of sense." Thus, we could say that a contextualist description or a description of a historical entity cast in a contextualist mode provides understanding of it by composing a verbal image of the relationship(s) existing between that entity and the "situation" in which it abides and has a specific function. Therefore, the meaning of any given verbal image and a fortiori of any description of the world or part of it can be of two kinds: contextualist when the description refers to or mirrors or mimics a relation between an agent, agency, or event and the situation in which it has arisen; and semantic or intersemiotic, when meaning is produced by intralinguistic (grammatical, rhetorical, poetic, dictional) exchange or the arbitrary substitution of signifiers of one sign-system for signifieds of another and vice versa, as in poetic, oratorical, or simply "playful" speech and writing.[4]

One problem this tack raises is that the referent of the *context* of an event or an action in the past is as difficult to specify as the event or action itself. For unless one is willing to invoke a theory of some kind—such as the Marxist model of base and superstructure or the primacy of modes and means of material production over ideas and beliefs as causes of historical change—to guide one in the search for what is active and what is merely passive in a given situation, then the context of any given event can consist of anything whatsoever that appears to be *contiguous* with the *event* or with the agents presumed to be responding to the *situation* under consideration.[5]

The philosopher Stephen Pepper has argued that "contextualism" is one of the four principal "world hypotheses" generated by philosophers and scientists in the Western tradition of metaphysics and epistemology (formism, mechanicism, and organicism being the other three).[6] Moreover, he has argued that contextualism, far from being only one method or procedure for producing historical descriptions of past objects and events, is the method *tout court* of the ideology called "historicism." In other words, abstract the procedures and protocols typical of mainstream historiography in the West and what you will come up with is a contextualist world-picture (*Weltbild*) with all of the "facts" left out.

The interesting thing about contextualism, in Pepper's estimation, is that, like historical inquiry, it is not only *not* theory-driven but antitheoretical in principle. Which is to say that, much like historiography, its theory, insofar as it has one, *is* its practice of an ad hoc inquiry or research. This is to say that in historical research fixed on context, you use whatever you find in the archives and you write up the results of your research in the mode of a "report" about what you found in the archives revelatory of your targeted object of study or you compose a "story" that tells of changing relationships between your object of inquiry and its successive contexts over time. In the latter operation, which we can call the "narrativization" of events (i.e., casting sets of events in the mode of a story or *fabula*), there are strictly speaking no rules or methods that can be stipulated in advance of the composition itself. There are, to be sure, conventions, generic models, archetypes of meaning and significance, modes of emplotment, commonplaces, and ideas of "propriety" available in the culture of the composer of the narrative on which he can draw as it suits his purposes. But the composition of a narrative about real events (in the past or the present) is an *inventive* operation: sets of events in real life do not take the form of stories. If anyone thinks that he "sees" a story in the documentary record of the past, it is because the story has been built into the record by its composers or the composer is mistaking his own fantasy for an external perception. More likely, the historian looking for a story in the events he is studying has endowed those events with the attributes of a specific kind of story (or plot) by his initial description of them in his notes.

The description (and redescription) of historical *processes* is much more difficult than the description of a historical structure or locale. This is because historical processes typically display evidence of changes in *both* the substances and the attributes of their objects of study *and* the substances and the attributes of the contexts with which their objects of study are related as well. In the study of any historical place, one looks for elements and relationships that remain relatively stable rather than those that change or transform. This is why a logic of identity and noncontradiction can be used to control for consistency in descriptions of those things in history considered to be stable rather than changing or that are at least *more* stable than changing, like contexts. But a logic of identity and noncontradiction *cannot* be used to guide inquiry into the relationships obtaining among different phases or epochs of an individual entity's life-course or serve as a control on the rationality and therefore the realism of any given narrativized account of historical entities in the past. Part of the fascination with anything apprehended as "historical" is its appearance of its continuity in change and its change in continuity. Indeed, historical entities have conventionally been conceptualized as undergoing not only metamorphoses but also transubstantiations. Things historical do not "hold steady," do not remain "fixed" so that we can capture them, as it were, in a snapshot or painted portrait.

And yet convincing narrativizations of sets of historical events get written, are recognized as credible descriptions of the states of affairs of which they treat, get lodged in the canon of historiographic classics which serve as paradigms for what will count as "proper" historiographical practice, and come to claim an authority that transcends cultural and temporal differences as *interpretations* if not as explanations of why what happened, happened as it did, when and where it happened. In my opinion, this is because the historiography in question—works by Burckhardt, Ranke, Michelet, Mommsen, Huizinga, Braudel, Hobsbawm, Lefebvre, Bloch, Cantimori, Le Goff, Duby, and, yes, the Marx of the *Eighteenth Brumaire*, and so on—is composed on the basis of principles of composition more literary and discursive than either commonsensical or scientific in kind.[7]

This is not to say—as I have been accused of saying more than once—that the great classics of historiography belong in the end to the category of *fictional* writing. *Imaginative* writing, yes, to be sure, in the sense that it is as much to the imagination of readers as to their rational consciousnesses that the great historians appeal. This does not mean that these historians dissolve the difference between fact and fiction.

It means that they dissolve the barrier—purely conventional, in any case—between history writing and literary writing. *This* distinction between history and literature and the taboo against any mixture of them in modern culture were based on conceptions of the nature of literary writing prior to the revolution in culture and society effected by modernism. Although modernist writing—the paradigms of which are to be found in the works of Joyce, Proust, Virginia Woolf, Melville, Henry James, Stein, Kafka, and so on—is continuous with the great tradition of "realistic" writing found in the work of Stendhal, Dickens, Balzac, Flaubert, and Fontane and is therefore marked by its focus on the present construed as "history"—which is to say, social structures in process of constant change, disruption, and revolution—modernist writing operates on the conviction (à la Giambattista Vico) that everything in culture is made by men and that not only history itself is so made but so too are the "facts" that comprise the knowledge men possess of their own self-making.

Of course, a certain kind of historiology was based on the conviction that a fact was something that one could "find" or "find out" by simulating a *visual* perception of certain acts, events, or constellations of events in the past. This conviction produces the genre of history as "spectacle" of the kind favored by popular culture in the age of video reproduction—as in the History Channel, the History Book Club, and the heritage industry. Here it is history which "dazzles," history which "thrills" that is on order. In spectacle historiography, the facts are indeed "fictionalized" by being deprived of their cognitive content and transformed into fetish-objects, engaging the drives, desires, and anxieties of subjects conditioned to live out fantasies of consumption fed by simulacra of "sublime objects of desire"[8] rather than by real relationships of intimacy and community with other, real people.

I mentioned above Danto's belief that a "fact" is "an event under a description" and that, whereas events belong to the order of things and material processes, facts belong only or at least specifically to the order of language.[9] This is why it can be said, as the late Richard Rorty was wont to do, that "truth" is not a quality of things that exist "out there" in the world and inheres in *them*, but is rather a quality of a certain kind of language use and a feature of language. Statements, propositions, or utterances can be true or false or neither or both. But of things we would not ask if they are true or false, for here we are interested in what they are and what they may mean in combination or collection. It is their reality that is at issue, not their truth or falsity. We may want to make true statements about them, but the truth in question is more semantic than epistemological.[10] We are just as interested in what they were and what they meant in the contexts in which they once acted and suffered and had their being.

But, at the same time, we must conjure with the fact that statements, predications, and discourses belong to the class of *things* written or spoken, of which it is legitimate to ask not only whether they are real or only imagined but also whether they are true, or contain truths, or have the feature of truthfulness.[11] And this brings us back to the problem of whether there can be *descriptions* of things no longer open to perception (because they are past and are known to have existed only by their "remains" or vestiges in the present) which can nonetheless be judged to be true or false in any scientific *or* factual sense.

At this point I would like to indicate that not all descriptions of complex phenomena invite judgments as to their truth or falsity so much as, rather, to some other kind of *adequatio rei et intellectus* (adequacy of things to intellect). In the West, the truth of propositions about the world has been conventionally assessed by appeal to criteria of correspondence and/or coherence. These alternatives suggest the two kinds of relationships between signs and their referents differentiated by Charles Sanders Peirce as iconic and symbolic respectively.[12] As images, descriptions can be said to bear some kind of *mimetic* relationship to their referents: they may more or less "resemble" the structures or the attributes of their referents; but in the case of representations which have no referents that could be inspected by observation or measurement, as is the case with past objects, it is difficult to conceive of what a historical description could be said to be a description *of*. So if we use semiotic conceptions of the sign-referent relationship, we will not wish to consider them to be either indexically or iconologically related. As a result, from a semiotic perspective, the prospects for basing the truth of descriptions of historical phenomena do not look good.

It is in the face of this problem that many theorists have fallen back on a "coherence" model for testing the truth or falsity of historical descriptions. On this view of the matter, the truth of a given description of a historical entity or process has to be determined on the basis of an analysis of the *logical* consistency obtaining among the various propositions (predications) that make up the whole of the discourse in which the description is presented. And here the "logic" in question is that of identity and noncontradiction which requires that the elements of the description be first translated into concepts and then correlated as an "argument about" the referent rather than as a *representation* of it.

But this is already to abandon the ground on which the claims for the *representational* nature of the truth claims of a description of things historical might be founded.

So let us back up a bit. If the pertinence of a description of a historical entity depends upon a representation of its relationships to its context(s), and this representation depends in turn less upon established rules and procedures for determining these relationships as they obtain in a specific (or as it is said, concrete) time and place in "history," rather than upon the improvisation of such rules and procedures appropriate for the description of individual (which is to say, individualiz*able*) situations in the past, then it seems obvious to me that the techniques and protocols for establishing these relationships will have to be more "poetic," which is to say, *figurative and tropical*, rather than conceptual and logical, in kind. They will have to be improvised and, as it were, "bricolated" in the process of analyzing the documents and monuments relating to *the* situation under investigation—so that the result will be a description whose "coherence" and "consistency" are those of a *symbolic* rather than of an indexical or iconic kind.

The philosopher Louis O. Mink has argued that the truth of a narrative account of a real set of events is not to be determined by the truth of the individual propositions that may comprise it taken *distributively*. And this is because, as we all know, even the greatest historian text will contain errors of fact or misstatement or misconstrual of evidence at some point in its enunciation. On the contrary, Mink argued or rather implied, the truth (or, if one wishes, the realism) of a narrative account of some part of the past resides in the sense it generates of a whole which is not so much "greater" than the sum of its parts as rather "other" than what it asserts or seems to assert on the *literal* level of its elaboration. But to say that the truth or meaning of a historical account cast in the mode of a narrative is greater or other than the sum of its individual statements taken distributively is to posit meaning and truth as *relational* rather than causal or structural.

Which suggests that the sign systems brought together and composed as a narrative description of some part of historical reality might be understood to consist of symbols rather than only of indices and icons of the things to which they refer.

In other words, the truth of a description of anything considered to have existed in the past or in history is *symbolic* truth. This means that a description of a referent in terms of the systems of symbols shared by a given community for the endowment of things and events considered to be "true" in the sense of "having actually occurred" with *meaning* or what, in this case, amounts to the same thing, with *value*, is and can only be a symbolic description. In this sense, descriptions of any given past or a part thereof deemed to be "historical" in kind—and whether produced by professional historians or amateurs, novelists, antiquarians, poets, biographers, romancers, or social scientists—partake of that activity of human self-making in which and by which human beings constitute or seek to contribute to the constitution of their identities as members of groups whose modes of affiliation are experienced as being *both* symbolic (legal, customary, and conventional), on the one side, and material (i.e., genetic or genealogical), on the other.[13]

Now, a symbol is a sign whose signifier is a verbal, visual, auditory, or haptic *image* (such as a circle or a cross or the words "circle" or "cross") and whose signified refers to other images of things considered to be of distinct positive or negative value by the culture in which they circulate as carriers of meaning. Thus, the word "cross" and the image "X" refer not only to a quadrivium or the Greek letter chi but also to a particular scene in Christian lore in which the Christian God in the form of the man Jesus undergoes a sacrificial death on a cross which, by its association with that event, acquires the value of "sanctity" wherever it appears in proximity with other symbols of Christian meanings or values. So, too, the inscription of a sign of the cross in any scene of the most banal occurrences can have the effect of transforming the meaning conveyed by the description of the rest of the scene in symbolic or only parasymbolic code.

Of course, in this example, the signifieds of a religious kind are *manifestly* symbolic and function to endow things with meanings on the basis of a shared identity of substance between the sign and its referent, on the one side, and its semantic content, on the other. But the same thing happens with putatively secular or nonreligious sign systems, wherein a thing or scene is endowed with value simply by the in-scription within a de-scription of it; it will have the effect of endowing it with a value, say, of "nobility" by the use of a sign such as a "white plume" or the arms of a gentleman (a sword, say) versus those of a villain (a dirk) or of a peasant (a club or ax). "To mean" or to have meaning is to manifest the attributes of or have one's "proper" in the things and scenes that are good, true, beautiful, noble, light, pure, and esteemed by the virtuous of the world. Needless to say, the meaning of a thing or scene may also consist in the opposites of the foregoing set of values. The important point is that although one can "explain" any worldly phenomenon *without* assigning a value to it, it is impossible to *describe* anything without also assigning a value or set of values to it.

This is because natural languages consist of mixtures of technical and common signs fraught with symbolic meanings. This is especially the case with the class of signs known as deictics, or locators of things in terms of conceptual pairs that have no meaning apart from their relation to the time and place of their use in discourse or their antithetical relation to one another: here/there, now/then, near/far, high/low, early/late, full/empty, part/whole, noble/base, good/evil, and so on. What happens in a description is that a thing or scene or event is successively redescribed in such a way as to be progressively endowed with a substance or essence worthy of bearing a Proper Name. The principal technique is called "adjectivization" or the identification of a thing by the number of adjectives and adverbs that can be convincingly applied to it and its actions. Thus, description can succeed in producing an explanation-effect by progressively revealing or uncovering the putative substance that unites all of the attributes of a thing to make it seem to be *this* kind of thing rather than some other kind. And in the indication of a thing's belonging to this class, genus, or species rather than to that one, value has replaced fact completely.

CHAPTER 5

Historical Discourse and Literary Theory

Is it possible or, if possible, is it desirable to "narrate the Holocaust"? This was the question posed to a group of scholars in spring 2011 in Jena, by the Institute for Contemporary History. I wished to approach the question from within the context of a distinction drawn by the philosopher Michael Oakeshott, between the "historical past" and the "practical past." Oakeshott was concerned with the reasons why scholars, intellectuals, and ordinary people turn to the past as an object of interest, of research, and of a knowledge that might be used for "practical" as well as "theoretical" purposes in daily life. He pointed out that historians were in principle interested in the past as an object of scientific study, motivated by a desire to determine what had really happened in discrete domains of the past, according to agreed-upon rules of inquiry, representation, and explanation. This meant, among other things, that historians wrote for other historians rather than for the laity, participated in mapping out that part of the past that could be accessed by way of documents and monuments, and had no other aim or purpose than to add to the body of scientific knowledge that could be assembled according to the rules of historical research prevailing at a given time and place. Other people were interested in and might turn to the past as an object of study for reasons more "practical" than "theoretical." Anyone confronted by a problem in the course of an ordinary (or indeed even an extraordinary) day might turn to his own past or the past of the community to which he belonged to dredge up some information, some way of solving a problem or simply identifying the *kind* of problem with which he was confronted—utilitarian, ethical, technical, personal, as the case might be—prior to taking action to solve it. It was this past that Oakeshott called "practical," and it was this past that was the object of both philosophers of history (such as Hegel and Marx) and ordinary citizens, politicians, and schoolmasters who naively thought that the past could yield knowledge of a practical as well as of a theoretical kind.

I understand Oakeshott to have understood the term "practical" in the way that Immanuel Kant proposed in his second critique, the *Kritik der praktischen Vernunft*: that is to say, as knowledge intended to help to answer the ethical question: "What should I (we) do?" Certainly it is perfectly understandable that, in any effort to deal with this question, one might have recourse to one's (or one's community's) past in order to bring to mind an idea of that "I" or "we" occupying the "situation" calling for practical action of some kind. It is important to recognize that the past thus invested as a possible source of practical knowledge is not and cannot be that "historical past" which, in any event, is accessible only in the books of history written and published by professionally competent historians. What can I possibly learn about my own situation or how might I conjure with it from any genuinely "historical" treatment of events in the remote or even proximate past? Insofar as I turn to "the past" at all for aid in deciding "What should I do?" here, now, in this present situation, it is a past which I (or the community with which I identify) believe to be most relevant to my inquiries. It is this past, rather than the historical one, that requires a narrative which, in one way or another, connects my present and that of my community to an existential present in which judgment and decision about the question, "What should I do?" are called for. What I require or at least might profit from is a narrative, a story which relates my present to that part of the past in which historians have little interest because that part of the past lacks "historicity."

Now, I suggest that the historiography of the Holocaust over the last half-century or so can be legitimately construed as having been suspended between at least two different conceptions or ideas of the past, one historical, the other practical, between which there is little possibility of cognitively responsible reconciliation. This may be one reason why a conference was held in Jena, Germany in June 2011 to discuss once more such questions as "Can the Holocaust be narrated?" "Should the Holocaust be narrated?" "If so, what is the proper mode, manner, or means to be used in its narration?" "What is the evidentiary status of survivor testimony?" "What are the ethical issues involved in the use of Holocaust images: graphic, photographic, verbal, monumental, and so on?" And finally: "What are the ethical issues involved in *using* the established facts of the Holocaust as an object of narrative or, indeed, any kind of *artistic* treatment?"

At the Jena Conference we were asked to focus discussion on two books: Saul Friedländer's *The Years of Extermination: Nazi Germany and the Jews, 1939–1945* and Christopher Browning's *Remembering Survival: Inside a Nazi Slave-Labor Camp*.[1] Both books are shot through with ethical as much as scientific concerns and indeed can hardly be seriously critiqued outside of an awareness of the conflict between a scientific and an ethical idea of the kind of scholarship that we must bring to the study of any event with the enduring relevance to our present world as the Holocaust. This is what gives to the relatively banal topic of narrative or, as I would prefer, storytelling, an urgency utterly lacking in the technical treatment of this topic by the discipline of "narratology."[2] Any decision to present the Holocaust in the form of a narrative—a story with a discrete beginning, middle, and end, and a moral from which we might seek to draw conclusions about what constitutes a proper life in any given community, and which, finally, seeks to render this event in terms that would "familiarize" it, domesticate it, wrap it up, label and "archive" it—any decision of this kind is not only shot through with ethical interests, but is in reality fundamentally an ethical problem and, moreover, an ethical problem of a kind peculiar to our modernity.

This is why I want to situate my own discussion of Friedländer's book within the context of cultural and specifically literary *modernism*. Let me offer five reasons for this contextualization. First of all, literary modernism—by which I mean first and foremost the modernist novel as represented by such exemplary figures as Conrad, Henry James, Joyce, Proust, Kafka, Virginia Woolf, Stein, and so on—is supposed to have repudiated any interest in "history" considered either as "the past" or as an object of scientific study, in favor of a kind of "presentism" that flattens out the difference between present, past, and future, inspiring a kind of epochal narcissism and killing any impulse toward a future-oriented and utopian politics. I want to suggest that literary modernism differs from traditional realism by taking "the practical past" rather than the "historical past" as its principal referent. Second, literary modernism is supposed to have abandoned what T. S. Eliot called "the narrative method" for what he also called "the mythic method" which is supposed to grasp reality in its abiding "essence" rather than in its temporally articulated "historicity." Such ideas have led Fredric Jameson—following Georg Lukács—to maintain that modernism, in abandoning "narrativity," also abandons an idea of history responsible to the lived "temporality" within which alone a "historically responsible" life can be conceived. In my view, however, modernism discovers the multilayeredness of the experience of time and temporality and seeks to present it in such a way as to shatter our confidence in the narrativistically ordered temporality of the folktale, fable, and "history." Third, I locate our topic within the context of literary modernism, because it is within this context that the revolutionary implications of the dissociation of "art" from ethics can be fully appreciated. This dissociation of art from ethics, the so-called "autonomy of art," is connected with the modern belief in "aesthetics" as the essence of the artistic as such. Modernism, however, repudiates this belief—it deaestheticizes art in the manner, first, of Flaubert, and then, that of Joyce, Woolf, and, in theater, the "learning plays" of Bertolt Brecht. (Compare to Eagleton, Rancière, etc.) And fourth, I take literary modernism as a context for the way in which it revises, not to say revolutionizes, the whole field of discourse, by deconstructing the myth of the omniscient (Homeric) narrator who presupposes that "he" knows everything worth knowing about the world he describes, that he knows that he knows it, and that he is capable of mimetically reproducing both the world and his own thought about it without significant error or distortion. Fifth and finally, literary modernism revises our idea of the event, so that it no longer has the crispness and perceptibility of the billiard ball struck by the cue ball and can no longer be plausibly represented in terms of linear causality. What I have called modernist events are "overdetermined" in such a way that they can never be emplotted according to the patterns used since ancient times to endow events with meaning.[3]

It is difficult to summarize a long and detailed "history" of anything, unless of course it is over-emplotted in the way the older "philosophies of history" or traditional narrative histories tended to be. And this is especially true of Friedländer's history of Nazi Germany and the Jews. Friedländer resists every tendency to emplot his history by presenting his subject as sets of (Benjaminian?) "constellations" rather than as a sequence of "scenes." For example, the text of *The Years of Extermination* is divided into ten chapters, gathered into three parts, with the titles "Terror (Fall 1939–Summer 1941)," "Mass Murder (Summer 1941–

Summer 1942)," and "Shoah (Summer 1942–Spring 1945)." The chapters themselves carry only dates as their titles (for example, "One. September 1939–May 1940"). These titles or nontitles have the effect of de-dramatizing the Holocaust, of refusing to allow it to be seen as a spectacle for viewing (in contrast to Jonathan Littell's historical novel *Les Bienveillantes* [The Kindly Ones]) rather than a catastrophe without form or substance.

So too for the passage from Stefan Ernst's "The Warsaw Ghetto" (described as "written in hiding in 1943 on the 'Aryan' side of Warsaw") chosen as the epigraph of the book and ending: "And they will ask, is this the truth? I reply in advance: No, this is not the truth, this only a small part, a tiny fraction of the truth. . . . Even the mightiest pen could not depict the whole, real, essential *truth*." This epigraph opens the way to a "history" written in a mode quite different from those composed by those authoritative narrators who dispose a critical apparatus that allows them to assess the evidentiary value of every source, determine its truth value, and elevate it or demote it as the case might require.

Or consider, again, the epigraph to Part 3 of Friedländer's text, "Shoah: Summer 1942–Spring 1945." It is a passage taken from the diary of "Moshe Flinker (sixteen years old), Brussels, January 21, 1943" and it reads:

> It is like being in a great hall where many people are joyful and dancing and also where there are a few people who are not happy and who are not dancing. And from time to time a few people of the latter kind are taken away, led to another room and strangled. The happy dancing people in the hall do not feel this at all. Rather, it seems as if this adds to their joy and doubles their happiness . . . (397)

What is the status of this epigraph? Does it contribute to an explanation of what follows? Is it a paradigm of the kind of evidence to be used in constructing that account? No, the epigraph is a figure which foreshadows the account of the events that follows, entitled "Part 3. Shoah: Summer 1942–Spring 1945." Moshe Flinker's image is a simile ("It is like being . . .") which casts a figurative meaning over the account of the events which follows, giving "constellational" rather than a conceptual meaning to them. Flinker's figure is "fulfilled" in the lists of deportations, shootings, gassings, mass burials, and cremations that make up the rest of the book.

Indeed, instead of a *sequence* of scenes of a drama, Friedländer presents us with a series of "constellational" images (again, I borrow the term from Benjamin). Each constellation consists of a number of paragraphs which sometimes add up to an argument or analysis or explanation, but at other times are simply registered as raw "data" gathered under a figure or image rather than a concept. These data appear as a *sorites* or "heap" of items which, gathered from different times and places and sources, attest more to the truth of what was believed to have been happening than to any "believability" they might possess.

In his introduction to *The Years of Extermination*, Friedländer also speaks of his desire to write a history of the Holocaust that would prevent "knowledge" from rushing in to swamp and "domesticate" the "quasivisceral reaction of disbelief" that must arise in the face of events that appear (and appeared to their patients) "unbelievable." What I think Friedländer is pointing to here is the new *kind* of event that was producible only under the conditions of modernization—for example, the difference between a pogrom and an "extermination." Modernism is a cultural movement which is founded on the recognition that modernization has made possible not only new events, but also new *kinds* of events—events that could be produced only on the basis of the new modes and means of production that capitalism in its advanced stages had generated: events of enormous *immediate* impact on vast areas and huge populations of the world, events whose occurrence was immediately transmissible throughout the world, events which, in the complexity of their manufacture, were precisely "overdetermined" and therefore could not be easily assimilated to the normal or traditional modes of representation, explanation, or emplotment. That the Final Solution happened cannot be doubted. That it happened is evidence that it had been a possibility in European society and culture long before. *That* it happened in European society and culture, when, where, and in the manner that it happened—this is what made it "unbelievable."

Such was the historical import of the Final Solution. Not its occurrence, but its incomprehensibility within the parameters of traditional beliefs about the nature of society, and especially a supposedly "enlightened" society such as modernized Germany and the European civilization to which it belonged. When it is said that the Holocaust is incomprehensible or incommensurable or unrepresentable, this does not imply that science or art are inherently incapable of comprehending them or representing them. It implies that we are using the wrong kind of science or the wrong kind of art—a science and art of a premodernist kind—in our effort to grasp the phenomenon in its "essence" as well as its "attributes." And the essence of the modernist way of confronting the modernist event is the recognition that things have no "essence," no "substance," that a failure of recognition is not a function of the techniques and devices of description used to prepare the phenomenon for "treatment" as a possible object of knowledge or perception or representation, but is rather a function of the non-nature of modernist events themselves.

For Friedländer, the Final Solution is not a product of a single line of causality and as such cannot be "explained" in the manner of traditional historiography. True, he posits "the crisis of liberalism," the role of Hitler, and the idea of "redemptive antisemitism" as crucial factors in the production of the Final Solution. But these are more in the nature of what Maurice Mandelbaum called "causal conditions" than the kind of "lightning flashes" that set off a conflagration. The Final Solution and its consequence, the Holocaust of European Jewry, appear to me to be presented as much more the product of the *whole* history of European culture and society and especially the modern version of it than as an aberration or atavism or "exceptional" occurrence. Indeed, on Friedländer's account, we can comprehend the Holocaust as a *possibility* inherent in European culture and society from its Christian beginnings, rather than see it as some accident or exception that cannot be accounted for by normal historiographical methods. It is its very normality that makes the Holocaust appear to be unforeseeable, retrospectively incomprehensible, and finally "unbelievable."

All of this has implications for the consideration of the issues implicit in the topic of "narrating the Holocaust." For if one means by "narrating" the presentation of the events of the Holocaust in the form of a traditional *story* (fable, tale, recit, etc.), which would include the older ideal of "historicity" informing both the nineteenth-century "realist" novel and the kind of "historicist" historiography inaugurated by Ranke, then all of the dangers listed by Friedländer in his introduction to *Probing the Limits of Representation* of 1992—aestheticization, fictionalization, relativism, and everything gathered under the title of "postmodernism"—immediately arise. Because it has to be said that the Annales's rejection of narrative as a legitimate instrument of *scientific* historiography—narrative not only as a carrier of ideology but as the very paradigm of ideologizing discourse—was perfectly justified.[4] Indeed, it can be said that *any* presentation of real events in the form of the traditional story, tale, or recit is not only aestheticizing, fictionalizing, and relativizing of the events with which it deals, it is also and inevitably dramatizing and (therefore) moralizing of them as well.

Thus, whether the Holocaust *can* be narrated and whether the Holocaust *ought* to be narrated are questions that arise as a consequence both of the nature of the Holocaust, on the one side, and the nature of narration, narrative, and narrativization, on the other. The Final Solution remains for many an anomalous event—at once surprising and undeniable, completely understandable in conventional historiographical terms and difficult to conjure with in what it implies about modern "enlightened" Western societies. In many respects, the Final Solution was the synecdoche of the Nazi program: everything in Nazism that was both new and old was summed up in this operation. The Final Solution was made up of a sequence of actions undertaken by agents as fully conscious of what they were doing as any historical agent is ever likely to be. This means that the perpetrators can be treated as the principals in a legal inquiry and as protagonists of a classic drama, the more so since, on the evidence, many of them had cast themselves in the roles of figures in a drama more or less Wagnerian from the beginning. The Nazis documented their actions self-consciously and at length. They photographed themselves as if they were actors in a movie, as if they needed a record of their "heroic" actions. Has any real event in history been more "theatricalized"?

The set of events known as the Holocaust (and its various synonyms: Shoah, Genocide, Destruction, Extermination, etc.) is a different matter. These events have to do with the fates of, the suffering of, and the destruction visited upon the victims of the Nazi program. The extent, nature, and gratuitousness of this suffering make of it—for many—a sacral event, by which I mean an event that admits of no "representation" and even less "interpretation."[5] The idea that the Holocaust could be adequately represented, much less "explained," by being emplotted as a story with a discrete beginning, middle, and end, a discernible "moral" from which we might learn a lesson, and a coherence that leaves no loose ends to wrap up and account for—all this offends against the feeling that the Holocaust is much more complicated and certainly much more difficult to comprehend than any traditional kind of story or dramatic treatment might lead us to believe possible. Not all fictions are stories, but all stories are fictionalizing of the events of which they speak. One can always tell the difference between history and legend, Auerbach said: in a legend things flow much too smoothly to be real.[6] So if there could be a story capable of conveying the truth of the Holocaust we could recognize it by the smoothness of its narrativization.[7]

Now, Friedländer's account of the Holocaust in *The Years of Extermination* is anything but smooth. One indication of its historicality is the roughness of its outline. It has been hailed as a great narrative account of the Holocaust; and so it is, if by "narrative" one really means "narration"; because modernist students of narrational discourse draw a distinction between a narration (an act of speech, invention, eloquence) and a narrativization (the "what is said" in speaking, a composition, a story emplotted as a recognizable genre—epic, tragic, comic, pastoral, farcical, and so on), so as to add meaning—usually a moral meaning—to what otherwise might remain chronicle, bare fact, or simple record.

Not all narration is narrativization. And it seems to me that what Friedländer has managed to accomplish is a narration of the Holocaust which resists the impulse to narrativize it, to wrap it up in an account of a process with a single or only a few lines of development, which point to a clear moral from which instruction can be derived for how to live life better under circumstances such as those prevailing under the Final Solution, and which allow one to label and shelve the event as "over and done with." And he manages to do this by using devices typical of the modernist novel.

One such device is that of "voice"—that of the author as well as those voices Friedländer summons up as patients of "the measures taken" by the Nazis to "solve" the "problem" of national contamination by extermination. I have mentioned Friedländer's careful avoidance of the tone of the omniscient narrator who is both "outside" the actions he relates (the objective observer) and "outside" the discourse (the objective judge) in which he relates them. On the contrary, he is inside the act of writing in the manner of what Barthes (following Benveniste) calls "middle-voicedness."[8] His writing alternates between transitivity and intransitivity vis-à-vis his referents (depending on whether he is speaking about the perpetrators or the victims) but is formidably "middle-voiced" in respect of his own discourse, which means that he is "inside" the act of representation in such a way as to be able to cede the stage to those diarists, witnesses, and survivors who wrote from within the Holocaust as it was happening.

Speaking of "the voices of diarists" that crop up in his work—and, indeed, do most of the work of interpretation appearing therein—Friedländer notes that "an individual voice suddenly arising in the course of an ordinary historical narrative of events such as those presented here can tear through seamless interpretation and pierce the (mostly involuntary) smugness of scholarly detachment and 'objectivity'." He then goes on to say, "Such a disruptive function would hardly be necessary in a history of the price of wheat on the eve of the French Revolution, but it is *essential* to the historical representation of mass extermination and other sequences of mass suffering that 'business as usual historiography' *necessarily* domesticates and 'flattens' " (xxv–xxvi; emphases mine). Note that it is to "voices" rather than to the "testimony" of diarists that Friedländer refers, what he calls "cries and whispers" rather than "statements" to which he asks us to listen.

Two things are worth noting here in our efforts to discern what *happens* in Friedländer's text, as well as what is *said* in it. First, the passages from diaries and letters, the anecdotes, the witnesses' testimony of pain, disillusionment, despair which interrupt the text—these halt the process of narrativization and, as Joel Fineman puts it in his brilliant essay on the anecdote in historical writing, "let history happen."[9] We are suddenly jolted out of our readerly concentration on the story and returned to the places where the events being spoken of actually occurred. These moments of interruption allow us, indeed force us, to take on part of the responsibility for the composition of the text taking shape before us. Second, Friedländer does not allow his own narrational voice to control our responses to these interruptions. The interruptions are not proffered as "examples" of a generalization or "instantiations" of a principle. They have the effect of a piling up of or aggregation of testimony which, though often differing in "content," typically conveys the "hurt" suffered by the Jews in their travail. "Niemand hat euch gefragt, es wurde bestimmt. Man hat euch zusammengetrieben und keine lieben Worte gesagt."[10] The effect of these interruptions has less to do with factual truth than with the truth of feeling. "[O]ften the immediacy of a witness's cry of terror, of despair, or of unfounded hope may trigger our own emotional reaction and shake our prior and well-protected representation of extreme historical events" (xxvi). Whence the pertinence of Friedländer's quotation from Stefan Ernst's diary ("The Warsaw Ghetto") to serve as the epigraph of his text: "And [people] will ask, is this the truth? I reply in advance: No, this is not the truth, this is only a small part, a tiny fraction of the truth. . . . Even the mightiest pen could not depict the whole, real, essential *truth*."[11] Such an epigraph prepares us in advance for something other than a well-formed story or an argument that purports to explain everything.

Friedländer seems to me to grasp this new condition of possibility for a historiography that narrates (in a mode or manner of speaking, with a certain kind of "voice") but does not narrativize—that, in fact, works to de-narrativize the events and things about which it speaks. He eschews the voice of the omniscient narrator, gives up control of the storyline, collects accounts of what happened here or there under rough chronological categories, allows things to happen that challenge our capacities to believe what our ears hear and eyes perceive.

How can this be done?

I want now to quote a passage at the opening of a book which I take to be a perfect example of a *modernist* treatment of the Holocaust, H. G. Adler's *Eine Reise* [The Journey] (written in 1950–51). This work, offered by its publisher as a *Roman*, has as its referent a real historical event—that is to say, the Holocaust, the events that comprise it, and the experience of these events by real human beings caught up in them.[12] The central characters of the book, the Lustig family, are all *figures* of the members of Adler's family, although they have been given other names and thereby transformed from persons into "characters" in a text. The events that happen to them in their journey from their hometown to a camp which is understood to be Theresienstadt and back were real events. But all of this is given, not in concepts, but in figures, in order, I would suggest, less to fictionalize them than to render them more concrete, more vivid, more accessible to the sensorium of the reader. *Eine Reise*, then, is not properly speaking a fiction although the techniques used to render it are the kind used in fictions to give an alien world the odor of reality. If we were to call *Eine Reise* a historical novel, we would have to specify that it is a historical novel of a particularly antihistorical as well as antinovelistic kind—like Tolstoy's *War and Peace*. In any event, here is how, after a brief philosophical *Vorzeichen*, this non-novel of a single chapter comprised of 304 pages begins:

> DIE ERZÄHLUNG
>
> Niemand hat euch gefragt, es wird bestimmt. Man hat euch zusammengetrieben und keine lieben Worte gesagt. Viele von euch haben versucht, einen Sinn zu finden, so wart ihr es selbst, die fragen wollten. Doch es war keiner da, der geantwortet haette. "Muss es denn sein? Noch ein Weilchen . . . einen Tag . . . einige Jahre . . . Wir haengen am Leben." Aber es war still, nur die Angst sprach, die konnte man nicht hoeren. Alte Leute haben sich nicht darinfinden koennen. Ihr Jammern war ekelhaft, so dass sich vor stellte, das war die Mauer

> der Erbarmungslosigkeit. Das Grinsen bleibt unvergesslich, es hat alle Muedigkeit ueberdauert und began schon in den zerstoerten Wohnungen. Eigentlich waren die Wohnungen gar nichte zerstoert, nochwaren sie in orderntlichen Haeuseren unter unbeschaedigten Daechern bestellt. Im Steigenhaus haftete die eingebeizte Geruch, der jedem Hause seine unverloeschliche Eigenart verleiht, solange es steht. (*Eine Reise*, 9)

> No one asked you, it was decided already. You were rounded up and not one kind word was spoken. Many of you tried to make sense out of what was going on, so you yourselves had to inquire. Yet no one was there who could answer you. "Is this how it is going to be? For a little while . . . a day . . . years and years . . . ? We want to get on with our lives." But all was quiet, only fear spoke, and that you could not hear. Old people could not accept what was going on. Their complaining was unnerving, such that around those left untouched by such suffering a cold and hideous wall was erected, the wall of pitilessness. Yet the tight-lipped grins remain unforgettable; they survived all weariness and first appeared in the ruined apartments. The apartments were in fact not destroyed, they still existed in regular buildings with roofs that were intact. In the stairwells the ingrained smells, which lend each house its inextinguishable character so long as the building stands, were still trapped. (*A Journey*, 7)

Who is speaking? We have no idea. Where are we? It is unclear. But one thing is clear: we are in a situation of threat and intimidation ("Yet the tight-lipped grins remain unforgettable; . . .").

And a few paragraphs on, what is threatened is revealed: it is the home. Here the narrator (whose voice is one among those of the "characters" in the "novel") tries to capture a family's feeling on the eve of its forced departure from the home that it thought it would own forever:

> They usually came in the late evening or during the night, carrying a message that cast its own terrible light: "Thou shalt not dwell among us!" . . .
>
> "Have you thought it over, my dear Frau Lustig? Tomorrow it's your turn. Off into the wild blue yonder. I heard it's so. I know for sure."

Blissful is the nonbeliever who hides the future's misfortune beneath the protective covering of the present moment, for now everything is obscured by darkness. No one *seeks protection when hope and silence alone mark the passing of time and make it believable. But in fact everything is unbelievable, anything that interrupts the horror. Unhappy belief! How unbelievable the bravery, how improbable the belief and all expectation, but in the apartment remnants of each are gathered. There they find old Dr. Lustig's medal for bravery, the letter from the regiment commander. It's unbelievable, but only the unbelievable can protect us.*

"It won't be that bad. One should . . . one could . . . He's done so much good! He deserves recognition . . . credit." (*A Journey*, 8–9; *Eine Reise*, 9–10; emphases mine)

. . . Now they [the "heroes," "commanders," "officials"] turn their attention to Dr. Leopold Lustig's household, which is to be vacated, though nothing more is sure. Even the officials carrying out their orders have no clear idea of the consequences of their commands as they scatter fates to the winds. A piece of paper brought along is taken out and handed over, the words themselves no longer important. Everything is destroyed, the bottle of raspberry juice falls over accompanied by a shriek as the carpet turns red. A weary hand reaches toward the bottle that rolls away after it falls and slowly lifts it and places it back on the table.

"It can't be all that bad, for it's not so far away, and at least we know where we're going."

But no one can sleep, the night is shattered. . . . for the living who follow the order for the journey to begin, there is no sleep, because everything must be relinquished. . . . That's what is ordered, and the main office won't worry a bit about what's left when those forbidden to stay leave the gutted houses. No one hesitates when the command is given, since it says in writing, "You are forbidden . . ."

Leopold, you must leave your house and Ida must go with you. Crippled hands and feet don't matter, the street is dry and there's no wind. So get going, there are no more houses for all of you to hide in. . . . Go and enjoy taking the streetcar from Stupart, because there is nothing left in this house that

> can still belong to you. That makes it easy to say goodbye.—But it was our house.—No, it was never yours, not anything in it. You took it all, since you paid for it with money that didn't belong to you; it was bribery that allowed you to enjoy the pleasures of your apartment. Four rooms altogether, a dark foyer, a kitchen, living quarters, a bath and toilet, cut off from the outside world because you hid behind a massive door with a flimsy bolt, as well as a dead bolt and chain to quell your fears, and a covered peephole, behind which a bad conscience lurked, climbing up and down the steps as if there were nothing to feel guilty about when away from your loot. (*A Journey*, 12–13)

This whole passage can be comprehended under the rhetorical figure of *kenosis*, the subtraction of what had been the distinguishing attributes of a thing. I have put in italics the passage on belief and the unbelievable because it introduces a theme that will extend over the whole novel. What are we to make of this passage?

The last words of Friedländer's introduction to *The Years of Extermination* are: "The goal of historical knowledge is to domesticate disbelief, to explain it away. In this book I wish to offer a thorough historical study of the extermination of the Jews of Europe without eliminating or domesticating that initial sense of disbelief" (*The Years of Extermination*, xxvi). This statement has puzzled some of Friedländer's reviewers: why would anyone want to eliminate or domesticate that "initial sense of disbelief"?

My dictionaries define "disbelief" as active rejection of a belief, as against the kind of indifference suggested by the term "unbelief." By *dis*belief, I think Friedländer means something like "astonishment" in the presence of something absolutely unexpected and frightening, and here the psychoanalytical concept of "denial" might be invoked to gloss his term "disbelief." Recognition of an event whose implications extend far beyond the circle of its original occurrence and threaten the cultural ego-ideal that lends esteem even to one's personal failings might very well evoke the response of "disbelief." It is disbelief in what the perpetrators did to their victims, not disbelief in what the victims suffered, to which Friedländer is referring. "I could not have done that. Therefore, not only did I not do it, but no one else has done it either." This kind of denial manifests an awareness that what was done in the Final Solution consisted of things both "ordinary" and "'unbelievable'" (*The Years of*

Extermination, xxvi). Our initial response to a "witness's cry of terror, of despair, or of unfounded hope" may very well "trigger our own emotional reaction and shake our prior and well-protected representation of extreme historical events," and our response of denial (of *dis*belief) is a means of affirming our prior beliefs about the "way things really are." But it is only if this sense of disbelief is recognized for what it is that we can hope to replace our prior preconceptions and prejudices with a clear perception of "things as they are." Science is one way to this clarity of perception, but art is another and, I would suggest, a more effective way; because in the poietic-artistic work the whole psychosomatic sensorium is engaged. In the presence of the work of art, we are forced to experience the many ways in which belief and unbelief, perception and conception, truth and lie, reality and fiction are mutually implicated in one another. Thus, when Friedländer takes as the epigraph of "Part 1: Terror," a phrase from the diary of Victor Klemperer, "The sadistic machine simply rolls over us," he is not only suggesting that Klemperer has found an apt figure for summing up what will follow in Friedländer's account of the period "Fall 1939–Summer 1941." He is also indicating that the account of the events to follow ought not be cast in the idiom of "business as usual historiography." So unusual and unbelievable are these events that they can be done justice to only in an idiom that holds belief and unbelief in a single image.

The presiding image of Friedländer's masterpiece is not a concept but a figure: extermination. From now on, it is this word that will be used to name what we have hitherto called "Final Solution," "Holocaust," "Genocide," and "Shoah."

To raise the question, "Den Holocaust erzahlen?" ("Can the Holocaust be narrated?") is to confront the issues of aestheticization and fictionalization of historical events and the ethics of representation of what Professor Saul Friedländer calls "extreme events." The extremity of the Holocaust has to do with "the measures taken" in the Final Solution to exterminate whole populations deemed unworthy of existence, of which European Jews were taken as the principal example. If "erzahlen" is taken in its "artistic" connotation as "to narrate," then the question, "Den Holocaust erzahlen?" asks for reflection on the adequacy of a genre and a mode of speech or writing to the "proper" representation of an event which, to say the least, is an embarrassment to the self-regard of Western European culture and society.

Quite apart from the historian's question of "what really happened" during the Holocaust, we are confronted by the enormity of the event's damage to the pride of our "enlightened" culture and the desire of many to insist that this event was an aberration or atavism of European history, that it should never have happened, and that its happening has to be attributed to a coven of gangsters and misfits which had nothing in common with the good, Christian, Humanistic, and enlightened folk who had made Europe into the leader of world civilization.

Of course, one can study the Holocaust "historically" without presuming to write a story about it or feigning to have found the "true" story buried in the documentary record and rubble of World War II. To study an event historically is to wish to set it within its original context, correlate its happening with what had occurred in that context prior to it, and map out the consequences for the context after the event had occurred. And one can do this without attempting to write a narrative or, as I would prefer to say, a "narrativistic" account of the process of change itself, which is to say, tell a "story" with a beginning, middle, and end, from which we might draw a moral or lesson that would help us avoid the recurrence of such a process in the future—presuming of course that we would not wish such a process to occur again.

Because to wish to have a story or a narrativistic account of the Holocaust is to wish to have this event rendered familiar by being endowed with the attributes or features of one or another *genres* of mythological, religious, or literary discourse. It is to wish to have disclosed the "plot" behind or within the events which might allow us to treat them as at last "recognizable" as conforming to a story-type, such as tragedy, comedy, romance, farce, pastoral, and so on, to be able to attach a label to them and to file them away in an archive for future study, to have at last "understood" them so that we might both affirm that they had indeed happened but that, since they happened in "history," they no longer have any import for us as anything other than information.

This process of "domestication," which Friedländer himself seems to regard as inherent in a purely scientific approach to the study of the Holocaust, is a danger—if a danger it be—especially present in a narrative or narrativistic account of anything. And yet, insofar as storytelling or narrativizing is an art-form, it must possess the power to defamiliarize, dedomesticate, or, to use a term in bad odor at the moment, deconstruct the images of reality that it tantalizingly holds out to us and, at the same time, withdraws, absents, and renders strange by its manner of presentation. In its capacities, then, of both domesticating and defamiliarizing events in our past which we can neither dismiss nor fully accept as having really happened, narrative or narrativization provides means for confusing our senses of what is real and what is fictional, what we might wish to repress of our pasts and what keeps coming back and demanding recognition as something that remains both past *and* present in our consciousnesses. But when it is a matter of finding a way to sublimate our sense of "a past that won't go away," it may be necessary to narrativize and to de-narrativize it at one and the same time.

Jean Laplanche thinks that we deal with the *Nachträglich* in a labor of constant translation and retranslation, until we find an idiom that allows us to construct an image of the past with which we can live well enough to get through the day. Such work of translation partakes of the ceremony of exculpation of our sins of commission and omission to which we cannot admit. In this sense, the massive labor of historians and others who write, unwrite, and rewrite our pasts has less to do with remembering the past than with letting it go in order to live a present life in anticipation of a future one.

This is of course less true of those who study the past "historically" than of those who wish to "to tell the story" of it. Narration, narrative, and narrativization are dangerous instruments for representing the past "as it really was." Stories have a way of escaping the control of their authors and of revealing more about their authors than they might wish. Friedländer knows this. And this may be why, some twenty years after he expressed a desire for a "stable narrative" of the Holocaust, he has himself produced an account of it which is not a "story" at all and hardly an "explanation" either.

What I have said so far bears the weight of two topics which have to be broached if we are going to take seriously the question, "Can the Holocaust be narrated?" These have to do with the philosophers' discussion of the nature of narrative considered as a kind of "explanation" of the events with which it treats and the disappearance of the traditional forms of narrativization in modernist literary writing and in the modernist novel in particular. It has to be said that the long discussion of narrative as a mode of explanation in historiology, which took shape with Collingwood and Popper during World War II and extended to the work of Mink, Koselleck, Danto, and Ricoeur in our own time, resulted in the conclusion that storytelling did not explain much when it came to the presentation of real, as against imaginary, events. As Hempel was fond of saying, historical narratives are at best low-level, "sketchy," and indirect "explanations" if they "explain" anything at all. So, it was further concluded, by Popper, for example, that historians might well continue to tell stories about the past, because history could not be the subject of a genuinely scientific analysis, and a "story" about the past was better than nothing at all. In the light of this conclusion, a desire for a narrativistic account—a "stable narrative"—of a complex event like the Holocaust would be a dangerous wish, for it would open up the event to all the kinds of interpretation that "fiction" could contrive.

Friedländer's fear that the Holocaust might be aestheticized and fictionalized by a storified treatment of it, of the kind represented by Cavani's film *Il portiere di notte*, could be extended to any narrativistic treatment whatsoever. So the desire for a "stable narrative" of the Holocaust against which to measure distortions and deviations in the direction of ideological special pleading or fictionalization was a two-edged sword. To want a narrative of the Holocaust was to want the aestheticization and the fictionalization of an event whose moral and political import was too serious to be treated artistically.

And this is where the modernist revolution in literary writing and the modernist novel—in the hands of Conrad, Henry James, Joyce, Proust, Kafka, Svevo, Virginia Woolf, Stein, and others—becomes relevant to our discussion. For, among other things, literary modernism repudiates—in its practice as well as in its theory—first, the aestheticist conception of the substance of art and, secondly, the identification of narrative writing with realism and the best way of representing the past "realistically." (Here I refer to the debate among Lukács, Adorno, and Brecht over the nature of "realism" in literary writing.) With the repudiation of the aestheticist ideology of art and the disidentification of narrative writing with realism, the modernist novel is licensed to abandon as well the "mimeticism" that had dominated the Western idea of *poiesis* since Aristotle, the idea that art was about pleasure rather than cognition, and the notion that poetry and prose were orders of utterance so different that they could not be joined or fused in the same genres of discourse. With the dissociation of art from aesthetics, it was now possible to think of fiction as merely one type or kind of literary writing, so that an artistic treatment of reality—whether past, present, or future—might be quite as "factual," might be quite as much about "reality," as utilitarian or communicative writing. The modernist novel is nothing if not fixed on the past-present relationship, its anomalies, paradoxes, and absurdities. It is simply that the modernist novel is more concerned with "the practical past" than with its domesticated (and, insofar as it has been narrativized, "fictional") "historical" counterpart.

APPENDIX ON NARRATION, NARRATIVE, NARRATIVIZATION

Modern historians tend to treat "narrative" as a kind of neutral container or form into which facts turned up in historical research can be decanted without significant effect on content. But modern narratological theory holds that narrative (like any discursive genre or mode) is itself a "content" in the same way that the proverbial bottle meant to contain new wine is already possessed of a content or substance even prior to its filling. In the case of the wine bottle, its content can be said to consist of the material from which it is made (glass, colored or translucent), its form (tall, thin, squat, round, square), its manner of closure (cork, wood, plastic), its labeling, and so on. So, too, in the case of a narrative we can view it as a form of verbal expression identifiable by certain devices, techniques, and modes of selection-combination which, taken together, generate the signified "story" and determine a specific semanticization discernible in a range of plot-types. Thus, a narrative cast in a "tragic" mode will make available a range of devices or markers recognizable as belonging to the plot-type "tragedy" which, when projected onto a specific body of events, actions, or processes, endow it with the meaning "tragic" rather than that generated by some other plot-type, such as comedy or romance.

As I mentioned earlier, prior to literary modernism, it was generally held that events and actions, agents and agencies in real life already possessed the attributes of specific kinds of events, actions, and so on such that their emplotment in discourse as one kind of event rather than another constituted something like the truthfulness of the representation. There were tragic events or sets of events which demanded a tragic emplotment. Mimesis was not so much a matter of imitating the external features of a given set of events as, rather, emplotting them in the appropriate mode and genre as dictated by their "substance."

Let me now lay out some aspects of narration itself. First, the question of narrative, narration, narrativization, and de-narrativization or anti-narrative in modernist and post-modernist literary writing. Here emphasis will be put on narrative (or narratological) form not only as a carrier or container of different ideologies but also, and more pertinently, as an ideology in its own right. By ideology I mean (following Althusser) "an imaginary relation to the real conditions of social existence" in a specific time and place. My argument is that narrativization, by which

I mean the imposition of a story-form on a series of real events, invites its projected audience to indulge in fantasies of coherence, completion, and fulfillment utterly imaginary in kind which may then function as a solace for the pain of the actual conditions of existence in modernist societies. The rejection (diminution, avoidance, abandonment) of narrative, narration, and narrativization, which is characteristic of literary modernism, then appears as a response in the domain of the symbolic to such fantasies and an index of a will to realism rather than that "irrationalism" which modernism is conventionally supposed to incarnate. The question which then arises is that of the status—epistemic, ethical, and political—of narration, narrative, and narrativization in historiography and whether the desire for anything like "a normative narrative account" of the Holocaust or any other complex series of events does not itself represent a desire for fantastic, fantasmatic, or delusory version of events too terrible to contemplate in their naked reality.

Of course, we should stress the differences among narration (the *énonciation*, the utterance), narrative (the *énoncé*, what is said), and narrativization (the arrangement of what is said in the form of a story). Narration has to do with voice, the tone and mode of utterance, mode being understood as presumed degree of mastery of the matters dealt with and the degree of authority presumed in the relation of the speaker to an intended audience. The product of this speaking process we call a narrative, the essence of which is also modal inasmuch as the narrative presumes a specific kind of relation to what is spoken about or the referent of the discourse. Finally, narrativization is the product of the mode of emplotment used by the narrator to endow the events chosen for presentation with a value of a specific kind—cognitive, moral, ideological, religious, and so forth. The endowment of the referent with the form of a story and moreover a story of a particular kind, genre, or species by means of emplotment produces the meaning-effect of the presentation.

Now, this conception of the narratological program allows us to discern the stakes involved in modernist writing's modulation, diminution, or outright rejection of narratological effect in a presentation of either real or imaginary events. Fredric Jameson, the most persistent theorist of the identity of historicity with temporality and of both of these with narrativity, has recently (in *Valences of the Dialectic*) adopted the concept of emplotment (as developed by Paul Ricoeur in *Temps et récit*) as a substitute for the idea of aestheticization to indicate the "form-giving" element (what I, following Northrop Frye, called "the element of construct") in the narrativization of real events and actions in historiography.

Jameson's revision of the idea of narrativism is based on a reconceptualization of the historical event as a product of humanly or socially generated forces which, in contrast to natural events, are or appear to be "overdetermined" in their causes and consequences. The idea here is that the historian's search for and representation of the causes of a historical event conceived on the model of the physical sciences is misdirected. History or more properly "the historical" is the product of an experience of a number of different kinds of temporality, quite different from the cosmological temporality of metaphysics and the existential temporality experienced by the conscient human subject. Braudel's multileveled structures of temporalities (geologico-geographical, social, and political) is cited as an effort to map the experience of "history" as an experience of the differences between, the conflict among, and the contradictions inherent in experiences of these different dimensions of historical being or existence.

My own notion of emplotment had been based on the idea that the narrativizer of historical events, in the construction of the narrativization, had drawn upon the fund of plot-types (tragedy, comedy, romance, farce, pastoral, epic, and so on) available in the cultural endowment by which to endow real referents with a specific kind of cultural (indeed, mythical) meaning. Jameson uses the idea of emplotment as a kind of "cognitive mapping" characteristic of the modern novel by which to correlate, colligate, or "configure" (Ricoeur's term) the different kinds of temporality experienced in such complex historical events as the French Revolution, the decline and fall of the Roman Empire, the Renaissance, or the various "crises" met with in the development of modern Western capitalism, including the advent of totalitarianism, the Third Reich, and the Final Solution.

By understanding narrativization as emplotment, the distinction between "factual" and "fictional" narratives loses its relevance for the determination of the relative "realism" of the various meanings with which "the past" or any given part of it can be endowed. Narrativization provides a key to the understanding of the attraction of storytelling over philosophical conceptualization of a complex set of events inasmuch as, in the novel, for example, "contradiction" ceases to be the "mistake" or scandal to logic that it is conceived to be in philosophical thought and is grasped as the existential situation of choice and decision which the protagonists of the narrative share with the prospective reader of it. The social contradictions of capitalist societies are multiple and ubiquitous, determined by forces impersonal, abstract, and global in kind, hence "overdetermined" to the extent that the individual must feel utterly unable to conceptualize much less conjure with them in daily life. This is why Jameson will argue that the novel is the modernist polyvalent genre par excellence, the genre in which, unlike in the romance, "emplotment" shows the impossibility in history of a simple overarching, coherence, and comprehensive "plot" or totalizing "meaning." No doubt, the modernist novel—in Woolf, Proust, Mann, Joyce—"pursued the mirage of unification which it still shared with philosophy," but with the advent of postmodernism (or late modernism) everything has changed: the postmodernist novel not only takes "history" as its manifest referent, but also gave up the search for an overarching plot or master-narrative and "chose to embrace dispersal and multiplicity."

Afterword

In these essays I have tried to expound an idea of "the practical past" and provide some examples of how this idea might be used to resolve some of the issues engaging theory of history since World War II. The fundamental problem of this period revolved around the questions of the possibility of turning the study of history into a real (which is to say, modernist) science and, beyond that, the desirability of trying to do so. As it turned out, the modern project of turning history into a science took the form of protecting it from a host of nonscientific or antiscientific practices: of which myth, theology or more properly theodicy, literature or fiction in general, metaphysics, and ideology were the principal kinds. The idea was to give up "meaning" (which usually meant "value" or "valorization") in the interest of truth or objectivity. But in the process, history had to cede its place among the moral sciences and its function as an organon of ethical reflection. The "scientific" status of history was saved but at the cost of history's demotion from its traditional role as *magistra vitae* to that of a second-order, fact-collecting enterprise. In the United States, the principal change in historiography was the shifts from politics, to society, to culture as a primary object of historical studies.

Nonetheless, history remained a relatively popular literary genre whose appeal among the laity lay in the putative *reality* of its subject matter: a past full of events comprehendible by common sense, representable in stories rather than algorithms, and seemingly linked to readers' present world by lines of a kind of genetical affiliation. In the twentieth century, history still served communities by providing a genealogical account of the formation of group identities. A history of a nation or a people, a group or an institution, provided the equivalent of an extensional definition of its substance or essence. The American people (an entity presumed to be quite different from the people(s) of the other "Americas") may have been an alien motley of pilgrims, castoffs, immigrants, and adventurers, supremely heterogeneous and vagrant, rather than homogeneous and autocthonous, but its historians could as if by magic demonstrate beyond a shadow of a doubt the ways by which it had transformed a "new" world ("a land without a people?") into its own and, in the process, had transformed itself into a new *kind* of people, superficially diversified but inherently one, noble, sovereign, and at home.

This genealogical function of historiography was quite different from the kind of research into the histories of families of an earlier era. In the older genealogy the aim was to show the perdurance and *purity* of the bloodlines of a given stripe, primarily to establish rights of proprietorship to specific realia, land and possessions handed down from fathers to sons of the same family. The newer genealogies began with the fact of land occupancy (however obtained, whether by contract or violence) and then proceeded backward to establish a genetical connection between the owner and the land. One might say that the new genealogies were "cloned" rather than found already given. That is to say, a legal fiction of a genealogical kind was established for the whole of "America" and the new proprietors immigrant from the Old World.

There *was* a genetic connection between the immigrants and the inhabitants of the Old World—as there would be a genetic connection between every new wave of immigrants to America and the various worlds from which they had come—but it was nothing like the genealogical connection between America and the Old World concocted by America's mainstream historians.

This genealogical connection is a perfect example of how historians produce historical accounts of the past which serve practical rather than scientific ends. A genealogical connection between generations provides a simulacrum of the substance shared by land, people, culture, and social system of a single historic totality. This is the social and political or, I wish to say, ideological function of "the historical past."

In drawing a distinction between the historical past and the practical past, Oakeshott provided a basis for shifting the burden of constituting a usable past from the guild of professional historians to the members of the community as a whole. With this distinction, the modern professional version of historical studies is suddenly revealed to be a theoretical, rather than the practical discipline it had been thought to be when history was regarded as *magistra vitae*, "philosophy teaching by example," and the linchpin of a secular *moral* pedagogy. And "the past" which the ordinary citizen carried around with him as an archive of experiences on which to draw for purposes of problem-solving, decision-making, and models of possible actions in the present suddenly returned as a legacy to own or renounce, without having to check the authenticity of any memories thereof with the historians who, in any event, had little interest in the ordinary citizen except as a subject of the state or a member of the multitude over which the state presided by "historical" right. In grounding the historical past in an existential concern and ontological basis connected with but separate from a practical past, Oakeshott freed the individual subject to take responsibility for the authenticity if not the truthfulness of a version of where one had come from, who one was, and what future one had a right to choose for oneself. This explains much of what is going on nowadays in what I would call "pastology": memory studies, oral historiography, witness literature, testimony, narratology, consciousness studies, species-theory, posthumanism, subaltern studies, and the like.

All of these had formerly been subordinated to the authority of the discipline of professional historical studies, forced to answer to the questions put to them by historians, forced to meet the criteria of truth and authenticity devised by historians for the scientific study of social groups and the individuals who functioned effectively in them. Now, the question of the authenticity of the experiences of the individual and the group-in-fusion, the kind of truth that was needed for the living of a life under conditions of oppression, want, and necessity rather than of freedom, opulence, and desire, and the validity of those beliefs based on experience rather than upon learning, all these come to the fore in the effort to take possession of, close with, and draw upon the practical past which the historical past had covered over by its own discursive practices and intimidated by the claim that it and it alone possessed the authority to con-fuse the true with the proper. For the professional or putatively scientific historian's truth purports to be the literal truth, a truth that is both clear and unambiguous, on the one hand, and proper to mankind in its substantive being, on the other.

Which leaves the ethical and utilitarian aspects of our desire for the past without a basis in being, without an *ontos* and an *ousia* in life. It leaves the practical past without a substance.

What, then, might be the substantive basis of the practical past? First, it must be said, the very fact of change and even that of development argues against any conception of substance as the stable noumenal basis of *existants*: mineral, vegetable, animal, or human. Unless we mean by substance something like the chemical conception of the substance of a chemical compound, then any notion of a substance of humanity, of history, of nature, must go by the board and be recognized as a construction by human thought and imagination only that stands in for the metaphysical noumenon we should wish to be able to name by the use of this term. Any notion of substance other than that meant by the physical science conception of it must, like the concept of identity itself, be recognized as a makeshift and placeholder for an oneiric vision of a life without death or a body without organs. Or a history without time.

Like its premodern counterparts, modern professional history promises to provide identity for the community, or rather, to provide community by providing identity, to name the substance that persists unchanged through all of the transformations that occur in the life of anything undergoing change, but to do this with a rigor and objectivity as scientific as possible. In this promise, history came close to providing a secular equivalent of the Roman Catholic doctrine of transubstantiation: the elements of the community were constantly changing as were the relations among them, but the substance of the community remained the same: identical.[1] But such a notion of continuity in change ran against the very conception of the individual on which the idea of *identitas* or self-sameness depended. Identity belonged to the individual—such was the ideology of Western individualism—never to the group: except by virtue of the sleight of hand effected in the genealogical conception of the historical past.

The psychological space of experience is not an organic but a mechanic space: it consists of fractals, fragments, detritus, waste, parts, and junk, none of which can be organically connected with anything else except by thought, language, discourse. How could anyone believe that the elements of a given individual's memory could coalesce into a coherent and self-consistent totality except by the violence of the "logic of identity and noncontradiction" which mistakes itself for the object of study it is supposed to regulate? The past of experience and memory of the individual is immune to this logic's aim to control. This logic has no authority over the imagination which works reproductively as memory and productively as trope. The imagination knows that the very idea of a *real* individual is a delusion. Moreover, it knows that it is this delusion which produces those lived contradictions that make of the individual life a prison to be fled from if possible or borne with a wholly gratuitous, Stoic resolution if necessary.

The so-called "performative contradiction" of contemporary philosophy is the normal condition of the individual in a group. We cannot but not fail to do what we say or fail to say what we do under conditions of society. "Must we mean what we say?" asks philosopher Stanley Cavell. It depends on whether you put the stress on "mean" or "must." If one means that what we say must not be *contradictory* of what we mean, or that what we do must not be contradictory of what we say, what authority does this "must" have over the productive imagination—the soul or substance of poetry?

Or, if one means that what we say must not be contrary to what we mean or what we do must not be contrary to what we say, it is quite another. For *being* against (*contra*) (a course of action, a person, an idea, a program, an order, or even a wish) is not the same as *saying* against (*contra-dicere*). And I can be *both for and against* a person, a thing, an idea, a course of action, and so on in exactly the same way that I can love and hate one and the same person or can be actively against and passively against a comrade or companion on a journey.

And so it is with the question of substance. The problem has to do with the idea that substance is changeless and stable, while appearances or attributes are always changing and transforming. Every historical entity—by which is meant any entity conceived to be continuous through change or changing in continuity—has to be conceived as changing on two levels of existence: appearance and substance. But if both levels are changing, then the very idea of identity (or self-sameness) must go wanting. This is one reason that the effort to establish an *identity* for a community of any kind by historical (genealogical) means must fail. Identity can be established only by an act of imagination in the service of the will-to-be as well as the will-to-exist. And this is where the practical past can be of service in a way that no version of the historical past can ever be. The practical past can be grasped imaginatively as a space of experience in which the would-be individual can contrive and substitute the illusion of substantive identity for the delusion of a self-identical substance of identity.

So what do we give up or lose in denying to the historical the potentiality of providing us with a communal identity functionally equivalent to that identity we aspire to for ourselves as individuated beings? What do we gain by imagining a practical past and putting it alongside the historical past as a contrary which is not a contradictory? First, we gain scope and extent for our inquiry. Second, we gain depth and height for it. And third, we gain an awareness of a richer array of conditions which have been experienced as the field whereon identities can be forged or fashioned.

After all, identity is forged of *acts* of choice, decision, and performance on aesthetic and ethical grounds (although I would combine these two kinds of faculty under the name of "practice"). Contrary to what traditional historiographers have suggested, knowledge of the past restricted to the kind which historians believe to be able to provide proof never helps us with the kinds of choices, decisions, and performances we have to make in our mundane, daily lives. First, because historical knowledge is always incomplete. Second, because it can never be adequately documented. And third, because it invites us to sink into a *mise en abyme*, an endless search for origins which may have nothing to do with the experience we are trying to take possession of as our "own."

Many years ago, Benedetto Croce wrote a book entitled *Teoria e storia della storiografia* (1917)—literally, "theory and history of historical writing." The English translation (1921) by Douglas Ainslie had it as *History: Its Theory and Practice*. You can see the difference. The original Italian title promises a treatment of "the theory and practice of historical *writing*," not a theory and practice of "history." Although "history" (events of the past, etc.) is dealt with, it is "history" as the referent of a particular kind of writing—historical writing—that is analyzed and *its* history recounted. The title has been changed in English in order to indicate what someone took to be the *substance* ("history") of the book's manifest subject ("historical writing").

And a similar thing happened to Croce later on: In 1938 he published a collection of essays entitled *La storia come pensiero e come azione*—literally, "history as thought and as action." The title of the English translation (1941) by Sylvia Sprigge: *History as the Story of Liberty*. And you see what has happened here: the English title indicates the *substance* ("history as the story of liberty") of the book's manifest subject ("history as thought and as action").[2]

Neither of these translations is wrong. It is just that instead of translating literal (grammatical) meaning, they are translating substantive (semantical) meaning. But in the process, they have figurated the titles of the two books, by which I mean they have employed the figure of substantialization (hypotyposis) to posit a "deep" or substantial meaning for the surface or apparent meaning of the literal presentation. But both titles manage to show how Croce himself substantialized both that historical world which actually had occurred and the quality of the kind of world in which a thought and action which were substantially "free" alone could produce a world whose substance was itself "historical."

But having said all this, we are still left with the problem of identifying the substance of "the practical past." Or we would be left with such a problem if we had retained the delusion that everything must have a substance within or behind or above in order to endow it with that thinginess without which it would fade into nothingness. But that fading into nothingness is the fate of all things whose substance is matter. Meanwhile, we need the illusion of substance—the notion that things do *have* substance insofar as we are capable of endowing them with such and treating them as if they deserved it insofar as they took up the challenge to act, if only from time to time and only relatively effectively, rather than to submit to the authority of those claiming the right to tell us who we are, what we are supposed to do, and what we should strive for in order to be at all.

Notes

PREFACE

1. Marie-Laure Ryan, "Truth without Scare Quotes: Post-Sokalian Genre Theory," *New Literary History* 29, no. 4 (1998), 811–30.

2. Michael Oakeshott, *On History and Other Essays* (Oxford: Blackwell, 1983).

CHAPTER 1

This chapter was originally written for presentation at the Universities of Tokyo and Kyoto, Japan. I would like to thank my friend Michiro Okamoto for his kindness in arranging these visits.

1. W. G. Sebald, *Austerlitz* (Munich: C. Hanser, 2001), 10; English ed, trans. Anthea Bell (New York: Random House, 2001), 4.

2. George Lakoff and Mark Johnson, *Metaphors We Live By* (Chicago: University of Chicago Press, 1980, 2003).

3. Hayden White, "Against Historical Realism," *New Left Review* 46 (July-August 2007).

4. See Erich Auerbach, Chapters 17–18 in *Mimesis: Dargestellte Wirklichkeit in der Abendländischen Literatur*, 4th ed. (Bern und München: Francke Verlag, 1967); published in English as *Mimesis: The Representation of Reality in Western Literature* (Princeton: Princeton University Press, 1953).

5. Catherine Gallagher, *Nobody's Story* (Berkeley: University of California Press, 1994).

6. This rogues' gallery of threats to the bourgeois family comes from Michel Foucault, *Histoire de la sexualité*, Vol. 1, *La Volonté de savoir*, part 4, section

3 (Paris: Gallimard, 1976), 136–39; and Eve Kosofsky Sedgwick, *Between Men* (New York: Columbia University Press, 1985).

7. See Hayden White, "The Burden of History," in *Tropics of Discourse: Essays in Cultural Criticism* (Baltimore: Johns Hopkins University Press, 1978).

8. See Hans Ulrich Gumbrecht, "After Learning from History," in *In 1926: Living at the Edge of Time* (Cambridge: Harvard University Press, 1997). 411–36.

9. Auerbach, chapters 17–18 in *Mimesis*. (Just because no one seems to think it important, I will point out once more that the subtitle of Auerbach's book, "*Dargestellte Wirklichkeit*," should be rendered in English as "*Presented Reality*," rather than "*The Representation of Reality*."

10. Reinhart Koselleck, *Futures Past: On the Semantics of Historical Time* (Cambridge: MIT Press, 1985), 21.

11. Jean-François Lyotard, *The Postmodern Condition* (Minneapolis: University of Minnesota Press, 1984).

12. For a survey of both the postmodernist novel in the West and the theoretical issues raised by the revival of the historical novel as a dominant genre, see Amy Elias, *Sublime Desire: History and Post-1960 Fiction* (Baltimore: The Johns Hopkins University Press, 2001). Some time ago, Linda Hutcheon pointed out that the postmodernist novel was given to the production of what she called "historiographical metafiction," which she characterized as showing "fiction to be historically conditioned and history to be discursively structured" (*A Poetics of Postmodernism: History, Theory, Fiction* [New York: Routledge, 1988), 120]).

13. Emily Sutherland remarks that von Ranke took exception to the novels of Walter Scott, on the grounds that they were historically inaccurate, although, as Curthoys and Docker remind us, he did grudgingly appreciate Scott's novels: "In his 'Autobiographical Dictation' (November 1885), a year before he died, Ranke noted that the 'romantic-historical works' of Sir Walter Scott, which found a reception in all languages and all nations, contributed principally toward awakening a participation in the deeds and achievements of the past. Scott was important for inspiring a nineteenth-century interest in history, and his novels were, Ranke admits, 'attraction enough for me, and I read these works with lively interest . . .' [But] he found himself 'offended' by the way Scott had knowingly created historical portraits that 'seemed even in particular details, to be completely contradictory to the historical evidence.'" See Sutherland, "Is Truth More Interesting than Fiction? The Conflict Between Veracity and Dramatic Impact in Historical Fiction," *The* And Is *Papers*, AAWP, 2007, 2.

14. Toni Morrison, foreword to the 2004 edition of *Beloved* (New York: Vintage International, 2004), xvi–xvii.

15. In what follows all quotations are from the preface to the fourth edition of *Beloved*.

CHAPTER 2

1. Berel Lang is the foremost proponent of the idea that the Holocaust is a "literal event," by which he means an event about which anything other than the plain truth ought not be said about it. In Lang's view, the Holocaust is an

event which by its nature precludes any ornament, poetic or rhetorical, and any "imaginative" treatment other than that of a reverence all but silent. He has developed, qualified and refined this idea with philosophical tact and ethical acumen in a number of texts: from his "The Representation of Limits," in *Probing the Limits of Representation: Nazism and the "Final Solution,"* ed. Saul Friedländer (Cambridge: Harvard University Press, 1992); through *Holocaust Representation* (Baltimore: The Johns Hopkins University Press, 2000); down to *Philosophical Witnessing: The Holocaust as Presence* (Lebanon, N.H.: Brandeis University Press, 2009). See also Isabel Wollaston, "'What Can—and Cannot—Be Said': Religious Language after the Holocaust," in *Journal of Literature and Theology* 6, no. 1 (March 1992), 47–57; and Zachary Braiterman, "Against Holocaust-Sublime," *History and Memory* 2, no. 2 (Fall/Winter 2000), 7–28.

2. Carlo Ginzburg, "Just One Witness," in Friedländer, 82–96.

3. I recently met a young historian who had been teaching Levi's *Se questo è un uomo* in a course on the Holocaust. He told me that he was constantly worried about how much of the text had been "made up" as against what there was in it of factual significance.

4. Todd Presner, "Subjunctive History: The Use of Counterfactuals in the Writing of the Disaster," *Storiografia: Rivista annuale di storia*, no 4. (2000), 23–38.

5. Of course, there is a great deal of work on the ways in which an artistic or poetic treatment of the Holocaust inevitably "aestheticizes" it, as if "aestheticize" translates to beautifying or making it desirable in some way. By the same token, some theorists seem to think that a "literary" treatment of the Holocaust will inevitably "fictionalize" it, as if literary writing equated with fictional writing only. The trouble here is with the ideas of "aesthetics" and "literary" that are being used. I take aesthetics to have to do with the effect of the perception of an object, scene, or event on the bodily senses and the cognitive weight of such an effect. By "literary" I would mean the use of certain identifiable devices, techniques, and symbolizations by which to endow things, real or imaginary, with meaning. See Ernst van Alphen, "Caught by Images: On the Role of the Visual Imprints in Holocaust Testimonies," *Journal of Visual Culture* 1, no. 2 (2000), 205–22; and Georges Didi-Huberman, *Images in Spite of All: Four Photographs from Auschwitz*, trans. by Shane B. Lillis (Chicago: University of Chicago Press, 2008), for another take on the "what is properly shown about Auschwitz" debate.

6. Immanuel Kant, *Groundwork of the Metaphysics of Morals*, trans. Mary Gregor (Cambridge: Cambridge University Press, 1997), 24–28.

7. J. L. Austin, *How to Do Things with Words* (Oxford: Oxford University Press, 1973), 150.

8. Austin, *How to Do Things with Words*, 151.

9. Roman Jakobson, "Closing Statement: Linguistics and Poetics," in *Style in Language*, ed. Thomas Sebeok (New York: Wiley, 1960), 353–57.

10. Primo Levi, *Se questo è un uomo*, in *Opere* 1, a cura di Marco Belpoliti (Roma: La Biblioteca di Repubblica-Espresso, 2009), 3.

11. The translators of this poem, Ruth Feldman and Brian Swann, use the English word "consider" for the Italian "meditate." I keep "meditate" because

it suggests the idea of "reflect upon." "Consideration" is a particular way of putting images and thoughts together, as in a montage or collage. A meditation might follow upon a consideration. Thus, I can account for the fact that the line telling the reader to "meditate that this has been," ends with a colon, and is followed by the words, "I commend these words to you." The imperative translated as "consider" by Feldman and Swann is actually "commando" which has the sense of "obey" rather than the English "commend." The anaphoric repetition of "Considerate se . . ." with its telling "if" is now "that"—the "might be" now has happened.

12. Feldman and Swann have "Disease render you powerless" for "La malattia vi impedisca."

13. Hayden White, "Figural Realism in Witness Literature," *Parallax* 10, no. 1 (Jan-Mar, 2004), 113–124.

14. Levi, *Se questo è un uomo*, 5–6.

15. Levi, *Se questo è un uomo*, 5.

CHAPTER 3

EPIGRAPH: Alain Badiou, *Infinite Thought: Truth and the Return of Philosophy*, trans. Oliver Feltham and Justin Clemens (London and New York: Continuum, 2004), 62.

1. Michael Oakeshott, *On History and Other Essays* (Indianapolis: Liberty Fund, 1999), 18.

2. Or dramatic process, by which I mean processes that feature conflict between human beings and other real or imagined forces, powers, and the like, the end or resolution of which turns out to be illuminable of the action leading up to it but in no way foreseeable from any given moment in the process as a whole. The plot types of the principal genres of Western drama serve as models of counterparts in real history, not in any fictionalizing way but because the kinds of conflicts they schematize are latently possible in the kinds of societies, which, as in the West, are capable of having "a history."

3. By "ideology of history" I mean the view that history is not only a science of the relation between the past and the present but uniquely adequate to the disclosure of the ways that humanity creates itself over time.

4. The same can be said of two other ways of representing historical processes in the West: the annals form and the chronicle form. Such genres may feature genuinely historiological motifs but do not add up to or fulfill the contract implicit in composition of a history. Cfr. Hayden White, "The Value of Narrativity in the Representation of Reality," in *The Content of the Form: Narrative Discourse and Historical Representation* (Baltimore: Johns Hopkins University Press, 1987), 1–25. On different ways of representing the "historical past," see the arguments advanced by Marshall Sahlins, *Islands of History* (Chicago: University of Chicago Press, 1985); Jack Goody, *The Theft of History* (Cambridge: Cambridge University Press, 2006), the title of which refers, Goody tells us on page one, "to the take-over of history by the west"; and Ian Hacking, *Historical Ontology* (Cambridge: Harvard University Press, 2002).

5. I am trying to introduce some Heideggerian language into the discussions about history, historical knowledge, historical consciousness, and the like: thus, I use the term "history" in the many senses it has in Martin Heidegger's *Being and Time*, trans. John Macquarrie and Edward Robinson (Oxford: Blackwell, 1962), in chapter 5, sections 72–77, and then use "historial" to mean "history-like"; "historiology" to mean the real, para-, pseudo, or pretended "science of history"; "historiosophy" to mean "the kind of wisdom one is supposed to derive from the study of history"; "historiography" to mean "the writing about history"; and so on, possibly, even to "historiogony" and "historionomy." It is a useless gesture, and I have no hope that it will be taken up in Anglophone discourse: first, because it is too jargonistic and, secondly, because it might contribute to the clarification of the term "history" and its various derivates, the vagueness of which is crucial to the maintenance of the myth that the term "history" designates something real.

6. The literature on "event" and "historical event" is vast. Every reflection on history ought to have event as a subject of discussion, and any reflection on history which lacks such a discussion is missing something crucial to the understanding of what "history" is all about. A useful summary of the issues involved can be found in Krzysztof Pomian's magisterial treatment of "evento" in the *Enciclopedia Einaudi*, which serves as the first chapter of his brilliant, but for some reason for the most part ignored, book, *L'Ordre du temps* (Paris: Editions Gallimard, 1984). The notion of "fact" as an "event under a description" comes from Arthur Danto, *Analytical Philosophy of History* (Cambridge: Harvard University Press, 1965).

7. See Hayden White, "The Modernist Event," in *Figural Realism: Studies in the Mimesis Effect* (Baltimore: Johns Hopkins University Press, 1999), 66–86.

8. Paul Ricoeur, *Time and Narrative*, trans. Kathleen McLaughlin and David Pellauer (Chicago: University of Chicago Press, 1984), vol. 1.

9. Alain Badiou, chapter 2 in *Infinite Thought: Truth and the Return of Philosophy*. The structure-event relation is the model most favored by contemporary analysis of the event in the social sciences. See William H. Sewell, Jr., "A Theory of the Event," in *Logics of History: Social Theory and Social Transformation* (Chicago: University of Chicago Press, 2005). Also: Mark Franko, ed., *Ritual and Event: Interdisciplinary Perspectives* (New York: Routledge, 2007); and Stuart Mclean, *The Event and Its Terrors: Ireland, Famine, Modernity* (Stanford: Stanford University Press, 2004), which has to do with the Irish famine of 1845 and afterward, an event which was known popularly as "the event" and inspired a lot of discussion about what exactly a historical event could be.

10. Paul Veyne, *Comment on écrit l'histoire suivi de Foucault révolutionne l'histoire* (Paris: Éditions du Seuil, 1978), 157.

11. I have not be able to confirm the existence of the term "archaiolographos" to designate an inquirer into the "origins" or remote past. The term was introduced to me by the historian Antonin Liakos, of the University of Athens, in an essay on classical Greek historical thought that is still, as far as I can tell, unpublished. I adopt it because I want to believe that implicit in the *practice* of the early Greek historians was an important distinction between the recent or proximate past and the remote or absolute past and that the former was the

proper domain of what later came to be called "historians." Bernard Williams suggests that historical inquiry is born when it becomes thought that the remote past, formerly thought to have been inhabited by various kinds of monsters, gods, fantastic heroes, and the like, as well as men, was suddenly grasped as being inhabited by people just like ourselves and was, therefore, comprehendible by the same principles of understanding used to understand ourselves. Compare to Bernard Williams, *Truth and Truthfulness: An Essay in Genealogy* (Princeton: Princeton University Press, 2002), 160–61.

12. Ricoeur, *Time and Narrative*, 208.

13. Although many modern students of Greek culture and language have set "mythos" over against "logos" as "story" might be opposed to "plot," "logos" rather than "mythos" is used by Herodotus and others when speaking about the "story" they are telling or wish to tell. In fact, many dictionaries give "mythos" for legend, fiction, or even lie (το πσευδοσ) and keep "logos" for a "story" which may be imaginary or true, as the case may be. These differences allow one to keep the distinction between narration (the telling or unfolding of the story) and the narrative (the story told, its "ending" revealed, and the connection between beginning and ending established), even though the Greeks tended to run them together and see their mutual implicativeness in the making of any given "historial" account of the world.

14. To be sure, "plot" has equivalents in German ("die Handlung"), French, Italian, and Spanish as "intrigue," "intreccio," "intriga," "trama," and so on.

15. Frank R. Ankersmit, *Narrative Logic: A Semantic Analysis of the Historian's Language* (1983), the argument of which is summarized, augmented, and contextualized in his essay, "Statements, Texts and Pictures," in *A New Philosophy of History*, ed. Frank Ankersmit and Hans Kellner (London: Reaktion Books, 1995), 223.

16. David Carr argues that narrative form is an adequate paradigm of historical sequences because human beings in society tend to try to give order to their lives, project plans, and act in accordance with narratological life scenarios (*Time, Narrative and History* [Bloomington: Indiana University Press, 1986]).

17. C. O. Sylvester Mawson, *Roget's Thesaurus of the English Language in Dictionary Form* (New York: Garden City Books, 1940), 166. Here after the entry "Event," under "Antonyms" I found only the enigmatic instruction: "See Destiny." Turning to "Destiny. – I. Nouns," I found: "destiny, fate, lot, portion, doom, fortune, fatality, fatalism, future, future state, future existence, hereafter, next world, world to come, life to come, prospect, expectation" and, further on: "Antonyms. See Event." I asked myself in what sense event could ever be considered an "antonym" of "destiny." And then it dawned on me that "event" was antithetical to "destiny" in the sense that the latter connoted not only "fate," but more generally "ultimate outcome" of a sequence of happenings, the individual units (or parts) of which were constituted in reaction or response to "eruptions" or rather "interruptions" exogenous to the chain up to the point of their occurrence. This insight, in turn, allowed me to see the probable relation on the semantic level of event to narrative, in which, as Mink and Ricoeur suggested, a historical event is a contingent occurrence which can be apprehended as having a place in a plot of (some) story.

18. Aristotle, "On Interpretation," in *The Basic Works of Aristotle*, ed. Richard McKeon (New York: Random House, 1941), 44–61.

19. Hans Rämö, "An Aristotelian Human Time-Space Manifold: From *chronochora* to *kairotopos*," *Time & Society* 8, no. 2, 309–28.

20. The "ohne Eigenschaften" alludes, of course, to Musil's great novel of the modern(ist) condition which is exactly equivalent to Heidegger's notion of the "thrownness" of *Dasein* into a world without qualities. Man the wanderer, the homeless being that desires a dwelling-place, is endlessly denied such a place because the world into which he is "thrown" is made of a space in which "places" are only temporary resting points for this being-without-qualities. See Heidegger, *Being and Time*, trans. Macquarrie and Robinson, sections 277–78, 322–25.

21. See "The Modernist Event," cited in note 7.

22. By postmodernism I refer not to the various forms of antipathy towards technological, industrial, urban, and social "modernization" which occurred in the West in the nineteenth century, but rather to the movement in art, culture, and intellectual life which in general reacted to artistic modernism.

23. Sigmund Freud, *Moses and Monotheism*, trans. Katherine Jones (New York: Vintage Books, 1955), especially part III, section I, entitled "The Historical Premisses." See also the analysis of this text by Michel de Certeau in "The Fiction of History: The Writing of *Moses and Monotheism*," in *The Writing of History*, trans. Tom Conley (New York: Columbia University Press, 1988), in which de Certeau treats the text as a novel.

24. Oakeshott, chapter 1 of *On History*.

CHAPTER 4

This essay originally appeared in the *Taiwan Journal of Culture Studies*.

1. Reference to Reinhart Koselleck on "space of experience" (*Erfahrungsraum*) and "horizon of expectation" (*Erwartungshorizont*) as the lived experience of the relation between the past and the present of a given society (*Futures Past: On the Semantics of Historical Time*, trans. Keith Tribe [Cambridge: MIT Press, 1985]).

2. An example would be a famous exercise in "cliometric" historiography: Robert William Fogel and Stanley L. Engerman, *Time on the Cross: The Economics of American Negro Slavery* (Boston: Little, Brown and Company, 1974).

3. The allusion is to the work of Mikhail Bakhtin which postulates a particular kind of "lived" or "practiced" time-space nexus as characteristic of specific genres of literary expression. The (modern) city, for example, would be one kind of chronotope while that of the colonial or "frontier" outpost would be another. Other chronotopes might be the classical *locus amoenus*, the sea traversed by the great steamships linking the metropolitan with the seats of empire, the (Greek) polis, "Siberia," and, of course, the concentration camp, the prison, the missionary establishment, and so on. Also see the essays collected in Mikhail Bakhtin, *The Dialogic Imagination*, eds. Caryl Emerson and Michael Holquist (Austin: University of Texas Press, 1981). In this view, genre

is conceived as more of a product of certain concrete practices occurring in a real place over a real time period, rather than as a literary form that could be projected onto a putatively "real" world or world of real things and thereby "fictionalizing" them. The genres of literature, which would include all kinds of prose and poetic discourse, realistic or imaginary, factual or fictional, would function as models or paradigms for the indication or description of events that could possibly occur or be recognized as actually occurring only in a given chronotopical site. A chronotope would correspond to what is *connoted* about a place in the German word *Stätte* (in contrast to other words, also meaning "place," in the same language: *der Ort*, *der Platz*, and *die Stelle*).

4. Deconstructionism, à la Jacques Derrida or Paul de Man, operates on the presumption that the two kinds of meaning—contextualist and semantic—typically "interfere" with one another, creating zones of indeterminacy or aporias that make it impossible to extract a coherent or consistent body of assertion from any extended body of speech or writing or determine what is being designated as "the" referent of a discourse.

5. The philosopher Michael Oakeshott has argued that the *only* relation historical events or entities can be said to have to one another is that of contiguity; see his *On History*.

6. Stephen C. Pepper, *World Hypotheses: A Study in Evidence* (Berkeley: University of California Press, 1966).

7. This was the burden of my study of the historical imagination in nineteenth-century Europe, entitled *Metahistory: The Historical Imagination in Nineteenth-Century Europe* (Baltimore: Johns Hopkins University Press, 1973).

8. The phrase is taken from Slavoj Žižek's book, *The Sublime Object of Ideology* (London: Verso Books, 1989).

9. Or as Roland Barthes was wont to say, "Le fait n'a qu'une existence linguistique" ("Le discours de l'histoire," *Information sur les sciences Sociales* 6, no. 4 [1967], 65–75.)

10. See Jerry Fodor for this distinction between epistemological and semantic truth: *LOT 2: The Language of Thought Reconsidered* (Oxford: Oxford University Press, 2008).

11. Bernard Williams, *Truth and Truthfulness: An Essay in Genealogy* (Princeton: Princeton University Press, 2002).

12. It goes without saying, I should think, that a verbal description of a thing is not an *indexical* sign of it in the manner of a photographic negative, because a verbal description is not in any sense "caused" by its referent in the way a photographic image is "caused" by the chemical reaction of light rays falling on a colloidal surface of film.

13. Scientific historiology may attempt to *explain* the development over time of this web of material and symbolic affiliations by developing some version of Darwin's theory for explaining the "origin of species" and "the descent of man" by random mutation and natural selection. Whence the current interest among some historians in the neurobiological and cognitive sciences and the theory of "cognitive evolution" which hopes to assimilate the historical phase of human species development to the story of its evolution. Here of course it is the "brain" rather than the "mind" or "intelligence" of the human species that becomes the

favored object of study, but more importantly this kind of "historiography" would seek to assimilate the processes of the human brain to those of the brains of other animal species. If this could be done successfully, it would mean that animals other than humans have their histories too.

CHAPTER 5

1. Saul Friedländer, *The Years of Extermination: Nazi Germany and the Jews, 1939–1945* (New York: Harper Collins, 2007); Christopher Browning, *Remembering Survival. Inside a Nazi Slave-Labor Camp* (New York: W.W. Norton, 2010). See Norbert Frei and Wulf Kansteiner, eds., foreword to *Den Holocaust erzählen: Historiographie zwischen wissenschaftlicher Empire und narrative Kreativität* (Weimar: Wallstein Verlag, 2013), 9–10. That volume as a whole constitutes the proceedings of the Jena Conference "Can the Holocaust be Narrated?"

2. Or for that matter contemporary pop and business culture, not to mention the U.S. State Department and politicians scurrying to polish their "narratives" in order to present themselves as persons who have something to say.

3. The point is made most perspicuously by Fredric Jameson, *Valences of the Dialectic* (London: Verso Books, 2010), 471.

4. Fernand Braudel, *On History*, trans. B. Sarah Matthews (Chicago: University of Chicago Press, 1980).

5. See Georges Didi-Huberman, *Images in Spite of All*, trans. Shane B. Lillis (Chicago: University of Chicago Press, 1980).

6. Auerbach, *Mimesis*, 21–22.

7. See, for example, Richard Evans's *The Third Reich in Power, 1933–1939* (New York: Penguin Books, 2005), a work of such consummate control of the facts and of such confidence in its knowledge of the Nazi phenomenon that it leaves nothing to the imagination of the reader. It is all so smooth that it has to be legendary. It is works like this that make one feel that it is the historians themselves, rather than the novelists and poets, who are makers of fictions. Certainly, the past never could have appeared to past persons as it appears to the historians. The historians find things that none of the actors in a given scene could even imagine.

8. Roland Barthes, "To Write: An Intransitive Verb?" in *The Structuralist Controversy and the Sciences of Man*, eds. Richard Macksey and Eugenio Donato (Baltimore: Johns Hopkins University Press, 1966); and Émile Benveniste, "Active and Middle Voice in the Greek Verb," in *Problems of General Linguistics*, trans. Mary Elizabeth Meek (Coral Gables: University of Miami Press, 1971).

9. Joel Fineman, "History of the Anecdote," in *The Subjectivity Effect in the Western Literary Tradition* (Cambridge: MIT Press, 1991), 59–90.

10. "No one asked you, it was decided already. You were rounded up and not one kind word was spoken." The opening words of H. G. Adler's "modernist" novel, *Eine Reise* (Wien: Paul Zsolnay, 1999), 9; English edition: H. G. Adler, *The Journey*, trans. Peter Filkins (New York: The Modern Library, 2008), 7. I wish to acknowledge the brilliance not only of Filkins's translation but of his

explication of the novel in his introduction to this book. Equally useful is the afterword by Jeremy Adler, "Only Those Who Risk the Journey Find Their Way Home," which documents his father's intention to compose a modernist novel of the kind written by "Joyce, Woolf, Faulkner."

11. For me, this epigraph raises the question of whether there might not be accounts of the past—in this case, the practical past rather than the historical past—in which the appropriate response would not necessarily be, "Is this true?" but, rather, something like, "Is this believable?" Or, "Is this an appropriate, ethically responsible way of thinking about 'truth' in the context of what Friedländer calls 'extreme events?'" I have tried to conjure with this question in chapter 2 of this book, "Truth and Circumstance: What (if Anything) Can Properly Be Said about the Holocaust?"

12. *Eine Reise: Roman*. The original was subtitled "Eine Ballade" and the mode ("Stil") of the book characterized by the author himself as "Lyrische Ironie." See the afterword by Jeremy Adler, 313. Adler is reported as trying to create a new genre, neither fictional nor factual but something logically and ontologically prior to this very distinction, something like what had been achieved, in Adler's view, by such (modernist) writers as Joyce, Woolf, and Faulkner. Jeremy Adler remarks of his father's decision to call the book "Eine Ballade," thereby creating a new genre, neither factual not fictional, for the presentation of what it felt like to be caught up in the Final Solution: "Ballade meint hier also keine traditionelle Gattung, sondern eine neue Erzählform, die zwischen Joyce, Woolf und Faulkner angesiedelt ist" (Thus, here Ballade does not refer to any traditional genre but to a new form of narration, located somewhere among [the examples of] Joyce, Woolf, Faulkner) (311).

AFTERWORD

1. Yes, I know that transubstantiation presumes that although the attributes of the bread and the wine remain constant, their substance undergoes change. My point is that the kind of change in continuity favored by traditional historians of the nation, the state, or the people is thought to resemble an inverted version of transubstantiation. Whatever changes occur in the attributes serve only to reveal the true nature, the deep unchanging nature, of the substance.

2. I have chosen Croce for examples of the substance-appearance problem because he was a great thinker writing under the press of a fascist tyranny.

Index

Adler, Hans Günther, 85–88
Adorno, Theodor, 92
Ainslie, Douglas, 102
Althusser, Louis, 93
Ankersmit, Frank, 53
Annales School, 48, 81
Aristotle, 8, 34, 55, 92
Auerbach, Erich, xiv, 11–13, 57, 82
Augustine of Hippo, 13
Austen, Jane, 11
Austin, J. L., 33–34

Badiou, Alain, 41, 49–50, 54
Balzac, Honoré de, 11, 13, 17, 57, 69
Barker, Pat, 7, 17
Barthes, Roland, 83
Benigni, Roberto, 28
Benjamin, Walter, 5–6, 12, 18, 78, 80
Bentham, Jeremy, xii
Benveniste, Émile, 83
Blair, Hugh, 10
Bloch, Marc, 68
Bossenbrook, William J., ix–x
Braudel, Fernand, 48, 68, 95
Brecht, Bertolt, 78, 92
Breuer, Josef, 58
Browning, Christopher, 31, 77
Buckle, Henry Thomas, 14
Burckhardt, Jacob, 68
Byron, George Gordon, 7

Cantimori, Delio, 68
Capote, Truman, 17
Cavani, Liliana, 28, 92
Cavell, Stanley, 101
Certeau, Michel de, 8, 12–13
Cicero, Marcus Tullius, 13
Coetzee, J. M., 7, 17
Collingwood, Robin George, 16, 91
Comte, Auguste, 14, 16
Conrad, Joseph, 11, 17, 57, 77, 92
Croce, Benedetto, 14, 16, 102–03

Danto, Arthur, 63, 69, 91
Darwin, Charles, 14
DeLillo, Don, 7, 17
Dickens, Charles, 6, 11, 13, 57, 69
Duby, Georges, 68
Dumas, Alexandre, 6, 13, 17, 57

Eagleton, Terry, 78
Elias, Amy, 7
Eliot, George, 6, 11
Eliot, T. S., 7, 17, 77–78

Ernst, Stefan, 79, 84

Fineman, Joel, 84
Flaubert, Gustave, 6, 8, 11, 13, 57, 69, 78
Flinker, Moshe, 79
Foer, Jonathan Safran, 7
Fontane, Theodor, 69
Foucault, Michel, 12–13, 20
Freud, Sigmund, 14, 58–61
Friedländer, Saul, 28, 77–81, 83–85, 88–92
Frye, Northrop, 94–95
Funkenstein, Amos, 6

Garner, Margaret, 21–23
Gass, William, 7, 17
Gentile, Emilio, 14
George II of England, 18
Gide, André 17
Ginzburg, Carlo, 28
Goethe, Johann Wolfgang von, 7
Goldhagen, Daniel, 31
Govrin, Michal, 7
Grass, Günter, 17

Hardy, Thomas, 11
Hegel, Georg Wilhelm Friedrich, 14, 16, 21, 29, 76
Heidegger, Martin, 54–56
Hempel, Carl, 91
Herodotus, 12, 43, 51–52
historical novel, 6–8, 17–18, 29, 32, 57, 79, 85
Hobsbawm, Eric, 19, 68
Hugo, Victor, 6, 8
Huizinga, Johan, 68
Hutcheon, Linda, 7

James, Henry, 5, 11, 69, 77, 92
Jameson, Fredric, 78, 94–96
Joyce, James, 7, 17, 69, 77–78, 92, 96

Kafka, Franz, 7, 17, 69, 77, 92
Kansteiner, Wulf, 28
Kant, Immanuel, 8, 10, 31, 76
Kantorowicz, Ernst, 60
Kiš, Danilo, 17
Klemperer, Victor, 89
Koselleck, Reinhart, 10, 91

Lakoff, George, 6
Lang, Berel, 27–28
Laplanche, Jean, 91
Lefebvre, Henri, 68
Le Goff, Jacques, 68
Lenin, Vladimir, 9
Lessing, Theodor, 14
Levi, Primo, 28, 35–39
Liakos, Antonin, 52
"literary writing," xi–xii, xiv–xv, 5–6, 8, 11–12, 19, 37, 56–57, 68–69, 91–93
Littell, Jonathan, 79
Lukács, Georg, 18, 78, 92
Lyotard, Jean-François, 17, 21, 53–54

McCarthy, Cormac, 7
Mailer, Norman, 7, 17
Maimonides, Moses (Mosheh ben Maimon), x
Mandelbaum, Maurice, 81
Mann, Thomas, 96
Manzoni, Alessandro, 6, 13, 17, 57
Marx, Karl, x, 14, 16, 21, 29, 48, 68, 76
Melville, Herman, 32, 69
Michelet, Jules, 68
Mink, Louis O., 53, 65, 71, 91
modernism, 7, 17, 21, 28–29, 48–49, 56–58, 69, 77–78, 80–81, 83, 85, 91–94, 96, 97
Mommsen, Theodor, 68
Morrison, Toni, 21–24, 32

Nietzsche, Friedrich, 6, 29

Oakeshott, Michael, xiii, 9–10, 42, 75–76, 98–99

Peirce, Charles Sanders, 70
Pepper, Stephen, 67
philosophy of history, 10, 14, 16–17, 21, 78

Pollock, Jackson, 20
Popper, Karl, 16, 91–92
postmodernism, 6–8, 17–18, 21, 53–54, 57, 81, 93, 96
Pound, Ezra, 7, 17
"practical past," xiii–xv, 8–17, 21–24, 42–43, 61, 75–77, 92, 97–103
Proust, Marcel, 7, 17, 69, 77, 92, 96
Pynchon, Thomas, 7, 17, 32

Rancière, Jacques, 78
Ranke, Leopold von, 13, 68, 81
realism, xiv, 8, 11–14, 17–18, 28, 57, 65, 68–69, 71, 77, 81, 92, 94–95
Ricoeur, Paul, 53–54, 91, 94–95
Rorty, Richard, 69
Rosenstone, Robert, 7, 17
Roth, Philip, xv, 7, 17
Ryan, Marie-Laure, xi

Scott, Sir Walter, 6–7, 13, 17–18, 57
Sebald, W. G., xv, 3–6, 8, 17
Spencer, Herbert, 14
Spengler, Oswald, 14, 16, 29
Spiegelman, Art, 28
Spielberg, Steven, 28
Sprigge, Sylvia, 102
Stein, Gertrude, 7, 17, 69, 77, 92
Stendhal (Marie-Henri Beyle), 13, 57, 69
Svevo, Italo (Aron Ettore Schmitz), 92

Taine, Hippolyte, 14
Thackeray, William Makepeace, 11, 57
Thucydides, 12, 51–52
Tocqueville, Alexis de, 60
Tolstoy, Leo, 6, 57, 85
Toynbee, Arnold J., 14, 16, 29
trauma, 25, 58–62
Trollope, Anthony, 57

Veyne, Paul, 50
Vico, Giambattista, 69
Vögelin, Eric, 14

Wilde, Oscar, 11
Wittgenstein, Ludwig, 4, 19
Woolf, Virginia, 7, 17, 69, 77–78, 92, 96

Zeno of Citium, 54
Zola, Émile, 11

FLASHPOINTS

1. *On Pain of Speech: Fantasies of the First Order and the Literary Rant*, Dina Al-Kassim
2. *Moses and Multiculturalism*, Barbara Johnson, with a foreword by Barbara Rietveld
3. *The Cosmic Time of Empire: Modern Britain and World Literature*, Adam Barrows
4. *Poetry in Pieces: César Vallejo and Lyric Modernity*, Michelle Clayton
5. *Disarming Words: Empire and the Seductions of Translation in Egypt*, Shaden M. Tageldin
6. *Wings for Our Courage: Gender, Erudition, and Republican Thought*, Stephanie H. Jed
7. *The Cultural Return*, Susan Hegeman
8. *English Heart, Hindi Heartland: The Political Life of Literature in India*, Rashmi Sadana
9. *The Cylinder: Kinematics of the Nineteenth Century*, Helmut Müller-Sievers
10. *Polymorphous Domesticities: Pets, Bodies, and Desire in Four Modern Writers*, Juliana Schiesari
11. *Flesh and Fish Blood: Postcolonialism, Translation, and the Vernacular*, S. Shankar
12. *The Fear of French Negroes: Transcolonial Collaboration in the Revolutionary Americas*, Sara E. Johnson
13. *Figurative Inquisitions: Conversion, Torture, and Truth in the Luso-Hispanic Atlantic*, Erin Graff Zivin
14. *Cosmopolitan Desires: Global Modernity and World Literature in Latin America*, Mariano Siskind
15. *Fiction Beyond Secularism*, Justin Neuman
16. *Periodizing Jameson: Dialectics, the University, and the Desire for Narrative*, Phillip E. Wegner
17. *The Practical Past*, Hayden White
18. *The Powers of the False: Reading, Writing, Thinking Beyond Truth and Fiction*, Doro Wiese
19. *The Object of the Atlantic: Concrete Aesthetics in Cuba, Brazil, and Spain, 1868–1968*, Rachel Price

Printed and bound by CPI Group (UK) Ltd, Croydon, CR0 4YY

07/07/2026